sex love yoga

dr cat meyer

if my poetry aims to achieve anything, it's to deliver people from the limited ways in which they see and feel.
                    -jim morrison

contents.

note from the author

sex.

love.

yoga.

a note from the author:

as a life-long, self-identified artist, i began learning how to create art at the precocious age of eight-years-old. it was in my blood to notice the finer details of my environment, while interpreting through the various lenses of my imaginative process. a beautiful mess of abstraction + realism, my work was constantly evolving, always incomparable to its preceding pieces, closely resonating with the flipping pages of my own personal journal. as i grew older, the expression matured. publishing my first poem in a children's book when i was in the fifth grade, i was so proud of what i had created. the effect that it had on my own internal world and creative process validated + forever changed me. thus began my lifelong romance with poetry.

from that point on, i kept a notebook solely for my poetic musings. it was a fuzzy blue spiral notebook, filled to the margins with gel pen scribbles about love + life, that in my youth, i had never experienced; of broken hearts + fits of passion i could only draw upon from what i saw in the movies! and yet, i was convinced that i truly understood these feelings. as i grew older, this fuzzy notebook turned into diaries, turned into blogs that no one ever saw, turned into beautifully bound leather journals, turned into social media sonnets, turned into poetic podcasts. poetry kept me sane + alive. through the traumas + the tribulations, the broken hearts + lessons that come with living, i lost myself to the page. poetry + art, my only preservers from going completely numb, became the threads connecting me to my inner world + life blood. here in the space of the artist, i could feel, cradle, and express this raw, unfiltered emotion while i transcribed to paper what i couldn't speak.

as i shared my work with the world, the reflections i received were often of amazement. viewers expressed their own projected recognition or meaning. it fascinated me that a single image could inspire infinite translation.

amid a world of intellect + rationality, we often seek solace in the work of the artist who recognizes our own story. music, street art, dance, spoken word-- we magnetize towards what helps us to feel. we then venture to make sense of these feelings by seeking out the teachings of experts in the field. turning to the world wide web, we scour content with the intention of discovering how we are supposed to act, think, + be in this world.

in our present day culture, we are oversaturated with content-- telling us the latest research + numbers of a general public that may or may not represent us as unique individuals. we are consumers of knowledge; absorbing podcasts, skimming articles, downloading books-- discovering experts on everything we never heard of, or could ever have even imagined. and yet, with all the knowledge we have equipped ourselves, where does it go? do we integrate it? or does it simply become the ammo with which we use to deflect + defend ourselves in order to not let the reality penetrate the thin shield of our ego?

how do we help someone to bypass the mechanism designed to protect us from a painful yet enlightening realization? we elicit a response of familiarity in one's thoughts + behavioral patterns that compassionately validates the experience as human; then ground the experience with psychological understanding. i am a psychotherapist by trade, an artist by heart.

i don't believe that the two are mutually exclusive. in fact, i honor when one can occupy themselves with both. that way, they can recognize people-- not as logical creatures, but emotive beings. while grounding our experiences, the science of human pattern helps to inspire us to engage in other ways of perceiving + thriving. existentialist psychologists like rollo may (1) + viktor frankel (2) believed that change in a person's psyche occurs when the therapist submerges themselves into their client's world, thereby discovering meaning in their current experiences, as well as their past history. for them, psychology + poetry were collaborators. they conjured the power of metaphor + symbology to help create mental connections + motivation in their patients by helping them absorb this creative, multi-faceted perspective. through the years, psychologists have acknowledged the specific importance of poetry + metaphors as productive tools in resolving some of life's more challenging moments. tom greening, a psychologist + poet, often wrote about issues he experienced in the field of psychology, focusing on the complexities of human thought + behavior. he even wrote poetry books as intentional attempts to manage his stress in the holocaust (3) + his afflicions to the the process of death among many others (4). greening's poems also found their way into major academic journals such as *humanistic psychologist* (5).

research, specifically on the impact of poetry on the brain + human behavior, has shown that the same skills we use to decipher meaning + formulate connections in poetry help us to develop skills of flexible thinking + holding multiple meanings that then translate to helping us navigate events + choices in our daily lives (6). especially when we consider the complex process of changing core beliefs + default reactions; our ability to slow down + question; or the pervasive challenges of considering alternative perspectives to our own programming in order to allow greater awareness + power over our decided course of action. for instance, we are conditioned to see a "breakup" as something to fear or something that is sad + hard to get over. yet a poem that depicts "breakup" as grains of salt acting as a catalyst to enliven something that is tasteless + dull, expands the previous perspective to include one of hope, perhaps adding "flavor" to our "plate" of life. an epiphany may arise from such a metaphor because it evokes the satisfying memory of tasting something after it has been seasoned properly. suddenly, it shifts our initial pain with the realization that this "salt" may serve to benefit our lives after all.

the research identified these skills as increased flexibility of internal models of meaning, enhanced interoceptive awareness of change, + an enhanced capacity to reason about events (4). an example of this can be seen in our conversations in which a person offers a different perspective on a scenario than the one we perceived. the more mental flexibility we have, the easier it may be that we mull over the opposing perspective to gain greater understanding or change our viewpoint all together. further, we'd have more of a connection to our ability to identify, access, understand, + respond to this process of change as it occurs within our minds.

it's my intention with this book to provide readers with a tool to expand their mind beyond the default inner working model in order to adopt a perspective that is more productive to their emotional well being. by presenting psychological themes in poetic form, i hope to create an experience that invokes recognized emotion + feeling in the body in a way that invites self-inquiry to inspire change. as humans we share some of the same pain, emotions, core needs and pattern processes-- which subsequently makes the reading + recognition of ourselves in poetic writing all the more influential. when we become mindful of the present moment + process (as is the intention of the poet), we are better equipped to extract the stories that are most alive for us so that we can implement the changes for emotional wellbeing that are vital.

sex.

as the divine intertwines itself.
the form of our figures.

on desire.

desire.
a most mysterious state.
spoken of as a rich, deep craving for,
attention to a longing.
that aphrodisiac to my tongue.
lustful breath from my lung.
returning life to a slow dying passion.
easeful when the contexts are right.
elusive when they are fleeting.

she moves towards us,
with seductive anticipation.
misreading our energy,
lost in lustful translation.
we freeze.
triggering her fear, confusion,
or building agitation.
causing her efforts to retract in hopeless self-deflation.

mental chatter infiltrates our minds,
portraying thoughts of shame.
shuts us down in quick submission,
dousing out the flame.

when two bodies speak in different dialects.
we write narratives of mismatch.
convincing ourselves this won't work out here,
and with that we detach.
we'd rather disconnect from our experience
than look at what is caught
avoiding all the internal assumptions
of brokenness that we thought.

- our hearts match where our bodies cannot

if you want to be desired, you have to take emotional risks.

we stayed up all eve.
whispering accolades to the stars.
their bright gratitude-flickers, reflected in our eyes.
and with that a sigh,
as i spoke of my leaving.
we embraced for a final goodbye.
and in that goodbye, my form instantly faded,
as it melted so deep into yours.
safe.
surrendered.
my internal state, off.
so quiet, your heartbeat cut through the loudest.

neither of us moved,
our breath became one.
energies dancing like embers between us.
dare i move a hand?
a foot?
my face?
paralyzed by the potential.
what consequence should unravel
if i take upon one look?
my hips come alive,
drawing small circles.
so subtle yet potent.
so erotic.
so bold.

your hand slides up my neck + in through my hair.
soft breath on my lashes sends flutters.
thoughts frozen mid spinning,
as your gaze here commanded
the most pristine moment i've ever--
twas the one 'fore that first kiss landed.

electricity built in that space in between.
with power to generate the sky.

a flash of lives + possibilities.
of love.
and of fights.
of promises.
and heartaches.
of sweet embraces.
and hard passion.
of magic.
completely sublime.

as our lips pressed in union.
the reality set in.
this friendship's taking a turn.
what follows,
only certain with time.

- *friends make the best lovers*

off + on
like a light switch.
this relationship drives us mad.
we hate them,
but we want them
as we remember what we had.

the ambivalence born from this internal conflict
incessant + confusing.
turns us into the compulsive addict
enticed by the intermittent affection of their choosing.
while the human desire for deeper connection,
fights with the reaction to self-protect,
a fundamental human conflict
creating high excitement
through friction they inflict.
as we resist
while we hold,
the entertainment of the fantasy,
intensity of the desire builds higher
an all consuming hunger.
transforming mixed feelings into one
single
focus on pleasure.
and to its power
we surrender...

unless our mind can convince our bleeding hearts
to channel our fervid energy elsewhere.
courting with disaster.
spawns an exhilarating flavor.
as we dance the line of what's forbidden.
we watch the fruits ripen
for us to savor.

getting high off the provocative scent,
derived from our hidden indulgence
of what's prohibited.
transforming anxiety into excitement
and the most magnetic attraction unfolding.
pressing into the edge,
the potential for something to go wrong
while riding the line of safety
as we break the rules,
our desires build up strong.

-the fight of ambivalence is a thirst trap

in the perfection + safety of the folds of our mind, it exists.
longing.
provoking.
inciting desire.

a projection of what could be
without the reality of the drama that was.
a fantasy of what it feels like,
or was like,
to be close.
handpicking all that was desirable while downplaying what was less.

our attention turned to where they are absent
or in our lives, a short supply.
we want what we lack.
we anticipate, looking forward to the time our bodies reunite
while filling the time in between with images of what could be,
what will be.

each dream depositing a wealth of pleasure with every thought,
every hopeful "how are you?"
every message received.
temptation to follow this rabbit down the hole.
led solely by our urges.

should the object of desire be a constant to our surrounding,
the anticipation is then built in the suggestive behavior,
the glances that inspire.
those *bedroom* eyes.
undressing us as they peer out over the edge of their coffee they put
to their lips.
or the brush of their hand to the small of our back.
sending shivers up our spine.
rousing our impatience.

desire precedes trust.
which is why the beginning stages of romance can confuse.
we may fill our minds with fantasies: "he's the one!"
or get lost in the hypnotic effect of sex: "it's so hot!"
we could spend all of our free time together: "let's be close!"
revealing our vulnerable tales: "it's so deep!"

body chemicals fuel the power of our desire, while the information
necessary for trust is still being gathered.
swept up by an aphrodisia lending so much of what we want– this
feeling, this person, this situation, this partnership--that when we
receive insight which does not correlate with what we need, we
meet the painful dissonance.
the part of us that desires, and the part of us that sees this does not
fit.
ambiguity.
taking up residence.
what is a bottom line + what can be negotiated?
the pain of staying in the question is often harder than the action of
the decision.

-but my heart's been waiting so long for her

the fear of loss can reignite desire.
at the edge where we find little to hold onto.
anticipation to the drama unfolding,
our fantasy spikes as our mind tries to play,
alternate realities that put anxiety to stay.

on fantasy.

'what do you want?'
a loaded question for most.
as the allowance of desire,
comes with guilt,
so engrossed.

we deem it
self-centered luxury,
a privilege to be so bold.
no space 'mid necessity.
yet for pleasure,
crucial to behold.

to know what we want,
what ignites us to craving
we turn to the images
our mind has been saving...

our fantasy.
to see what we find.
become our truest erotic.
for us to unwind.

living out another scene,
another persona,
beyond routine.
entertaining a lover
or past romance,
we recover.

we take offense to this play
fearing our desires unnatural,
not knowing what they mean.
as the stories are not casual.

likening to our traumas,
countering our values,
with our own dramas.
yet they activate our bodies

sexually alive,
igniting our fires.
so our libido can thrive.
that can only be extinguished
by the cooling effects of shame.
the poison of potential.
we indulge all the same.

so our choice here is to liberate
from this damning consequence
or embrace our whole selves,
as we move through this dance.

-to know what we want can feel like a burden

time rolls on.
the echo of the tick to speak of its passage.
i'm draped over the couch, imprinting my figure.
eyes roving the room, watching you flutter.
where your need for productivity fuels every limb.
what can i say that would magnetize you to me?
desire me,
no,
crave me.

my valley runs dry from the lack of your attention.
conditioned that she'll go untouched.
unsought for.
famished.

the pupils of your eyes dart across each page you're on.
soaking up every word.
what could i do to elicit a response?
erotic + passionate
to replace nonchalance.

a sigh escapes my lungs.
my lids close over this scene.
and i'm taken over by another.

she's running her hands through my hair,
nails tracing my scalp.
her kiss the sweetest taste of berries and ecstacy.
my body flutters with delicious resonance.
his nose trails up my inner thigh,
gentle bites along the way.
gasps escape me.
muscles contract.
succumbed by this duo.

time no longer speaks,
but swirls into voiceless tones.

i touch my own skin.
amid this provocative display.
over + over +over its played.
'til i crave nothing more than the sweetest release.

an unfamiliar hand.
or one whose touch is quite known.
my eyes flutter half an inch,
to the fiery gaze that you hold.
wordless in your expression,
yet speaking your intention
of want.

do i dare let this preceding naysayer into my bliss?
he smiles.
the most devilish of fangs.
the password to my frame.
head falls back in total abandon.

that desire.
that appetite.
the strong power,
taking reign.

what is a fantasy, except the illustration of your existence entwined
with mine
forever preserved in the folds of my mind.

the infinite characters i play,
for infinite storylines each day.
body + imagination do conspire.
conceived by my unyielding desire.

in a conversation-filled room,
his gaze spoke the loudest.
capturing mine like a green + golden net.
hypnotic.
the corner of his mouth turned up in an impish smile.
his fantasy playing on screen in the back of his mind.
and i the main role of whatever was unfolding.

i shudder.
not from the cold,
but from the internal conflict between my own pleasure fighting
propriety.

how much can i stand it,
before my internal principles shut it down.
i'm in public.
he takes one step forward.
i don't know him.
his chin draws up.
i'm good + self-respecting.
his lips part slightly.
i can't let go.
his energy pulsating.
or is that mine? anymore i can't tell the difference,
as the distance between us shrinks.
sagas of our passion flashed quickly behind my eyes.
improperly decent.
elegantly wrong.

into the host's study, we stumble with thoughtless action.
lips colliding as if to steal from him the last bit of oxygen, of life, in
this room. clothes feverishly removed + cast carelessly aside.
his effort parts my legs like a knife through soft butter,
as his fingers play music, a master concerto.

my legs hardly hold me to stand here in fervor,
his hands find their way around, holding my ass.
lifting my hips his strength pins me against the bookcase.
the aroma of old leather and pages get me high.

snap back to reality, the study scene fades away.
his charming face comes nearer.
i'm totally lost at what to say.
gulping down whatever knot had built,
getting lodged in the depths of my throat.
and with that, my smile greets his.
nodding my head.
i turn to walk away.
my skin is hot, conducting the electricity.
barely containing its pulsating power.

my highest desire to preserve this whole fantasy.
for with a single word breathed,
the fantasy would crumble.

-*"as reality is not as perfect as what we create from within?"*

self-reflections:

1. when i study the erotic fantasies that tend to cross my mind, what elements about them seem to be more frequent?
2. what about my fantasies would i feel comfortable about sharing with my lover + what elements would i not?
3. what beliefs or judgments do i hold about what turns me on?

on body.

the lines along her thighs read like poetry in the early morning light.
each one portrayed its own story
of pain
of beauty
of strength
of love.
as my fingertips traced the lifespan of each one,
i fell even more entranced to the character they spoke of.

the nectar of the goddess.
sweet.
nourishing.
silky wet.
like honey.
dare we taste our own substance?
as she seeps out in abundance?
we contract out of fear
the response of our mind.
dancing images of rejection,
disgust,
repulsion,
unkind words forming a lie.
"don't worship her with your tongue there."
"don't lap her up good."
the sound of our fear trumping pleasure,
with only a mere whisper
as we brush off what could.

who dare we give that power,
to be the author of our shame?
a misguided assumption.
and our something to reclaim.

my body confuses.
does she flow because she wants it--
while my brain tells me no?

-discordance

you paint my body.
your words like the softest paintbrush.
washing over my canvas creating art out of what I see as nothing.
i must be blind
or veiled to the exquisite scene you speak novels of.
stories of an exotic landscape.
lush + plump.
sweet + satiating.
easy to get caught in.
when your lips put life to those words.
i pray this artistry never ends.

"it's only you."
i whispered into your ear.
your glance turned to the side.
the same words could not be reflected.
i'm drunk on erotic chemicals,
stupid to any comprehension.
amid the throws of passion
and your body pressing so fervently into mine.
my lips said yes
while my body remained in quiet confusion.
a part of me shut down,
pulled away.
still a part ofme pulled you in deeper.

playing out my expression
between a split in my consciousness.
sabotaging my surrender.
to never reach that high peak.

after you left,
i lay in vast emptiness.
one in which i thought i was filling with you,
only to realize it was made by you.
or me.
the betrayal of my own integrity.
now i sit, alone in my body.
(the smell of you still lingering on my pillow)
observing the time i left her,
my body,
in harmful abandon.

to ignore our body is the greatest betrayal.
yet, how often do we push onward,
communicating to our body that it is wrong;
that we can make it do what we want it to.
only to be left feeling ill thereafter.

the conflict among companions can be painful:
-*how to resolve the mind, the heart, + the body who argue?*

on connection.

envious i was of the very air that had the honor of kissing her from the inside.
nourishing the very being that lay before me.

the formula for connection.
the ingredients we do have.
purest form of presence.
extended through our fingertips.
holding her with our attention.
the senses.
our body.

making love to the space in between.
our lips.
breathing each other in.
fingers glide the tops of her arm hairs.
as we taste the salt along her skin.

sexuality can exist without sensuality.
yet why ever would we?
when the juiciest of elements exist right where we live.
when we slow down.
tune in.
breathe in.
relax.

our body + mind open to the expansive world existing
just at the edge of our sensation threshold.

nesting.
that moment after sex
in which we stay here, connected.
weaved with our lover in the energy erected.
where we hold or are held,
witnessing everything related.
crying.
shuddering.
settling into bliss,
sadness,
confusion,
our own emptiness.

good sex needn't end with our bodies feeling elated.
sometimes our own animals
become tearful or agitated.
an intense concoction of hormones
leave us in confused disarray
as the physical release of climax
collapses the wall that had retained.

emotions + fears
insecurities + tears
flooding over in a rush
after being long held out
can leave us in confusion
and feelings of strong doubt.

yet to be held just for a moment,
staying present to what is true.
allows for depth of intimacy
bonded here with you.

snuggles: the all natural, organic, gmo-free medicine for the treatment of loneliness, depression, + cold feet.

on alchemy.

ask him:
how do you worship a goddess?

passion is practiced.
the pure enjoyment in the progression.
present to the meetings,
subtle touches,
contact of eyes,
buzz of the body,
absence of pushing for more...just yet.

holding here to this point,
reveling in the potential to develop.
the practice is in the savoring.
in the pleasure.
in the tease,
the approach to the edge + backing ourselves down.
to go it again.
building.
waiting.
anticipating.
fervor.
the palpable texture weaving vitality + wanting.
the wait both delicious + daunting.

to master erotic energy, we must learn the dance of yin + yang.
surrendering to the flow (yin) by breathing, relaxing + opening our
body.
melting into ourselves + the movement of our partner.
tuning into the subtle sensations as they are alive on our skin + in
our soul.
slow.
moving like water —
liquid.
doing less, while feeling more.
all the while, directing the energy (yang) by breath, sound,
movement, touch, + visualization.
breathe to ignite the inner fire.
sound vibration to break tension
circulation of hips to activate
present to the edge of resistance — where I press into you, I am met
with equal resistance.
not fighting,
but attuning,
that we consistently meet + are met.
consciousness in our fingertips as we play along the silhouette of
her body.
visualizing the expansion of pleasure that flows through.

like the river,
we cannot push or force erotic energy —
only surrender to the flow of its potency.

good sex is not linear.
it is a coloring page with crayon scribbled all over + outside the
lines.
thin lines.
dotted lines.
lines that barely leave a trace
and lines so bold the crayon nearly breaks.

in other words--good sex is felt + is moved by this feeling.
it is not a race to achieve the orgasm.
nor is it a neatly packaged performance drawn within the lines that
are socially idealized.
no.
it is messy.
it is loud.
it is soft.
it is a manifestation of our most authentic expression--
when we surrender to it.
moments of action followed by moments of gazing followed by
moments of laughter + weeping.
moments of experimentation followed by moments of passion
followed by role reversal + reflection.

good sex may not have an orgasm.
good sex may not ever penetrate.
good sex may not last long.

but it is the manifestation of our desires + needs
voiced.
a co-written song between lovers.
the primal expression of who we are
scribbled all across each page of our book.

-*my crayons are broken.*

on insecurities + fears.

to put me on top,
my mind goes suspended.
disjointed,
my movement
ease in expression ended.
shyness taking over,
as i fear my incompetence.
pressure in the role
for leading + control,
i abdicate this throne
to preserve my own mind,
let me surrender
so i can unwind.

-*bottom.*

to be the receiver,
i cringe at the shift.
patience lost in this position.
as my mind goes adrift.
give me the role where i'm in power once again.
the letting go is my contender.
for what do i do with myself therein?

-let me go down on you again.

desires play out like a movie in the back of our minds,
silent is the scene, as our own repression speaks over.
the conflicted sexual ethos:
inner drama enacted by our truth + the parts that oppose.
the yes + the no.
the good + the evil.
the proper + the perverted.
shame in the confusion:
what is the significance—
as we compare it to the imaginable lens of another?
does our attractiveness suffice,
to be deemed good enough,
sexy enough.
that we may permit our desire to fulfillment.

conversion from the mental to the physical
manifesting in corresponding muscles holding control
as we work to suppress the expression.
rigidity to our being.
clipping our own wings
limiting potential.

yet the faint monologue of our sexual truth still speaks
alive behind the curtain,
'til the entertainment of that one conversation can be realized,
received,
related with.
the start.
for now, stays locked up deep in our heart.

to be a human who loves sex.
we may be the receptacle to other's projections.
a fuckboy.
a slut.
a whore.

the cultural wounding
seeping messages of shame,
while saturating us with images of the idealized.
this is what it should look like.
these are the people who should have it.

no surprise there are secrets,
unspoken desires.
guilt-laden fantasies.
identities unrequited.

the fear of rejection is made strong.
shame--
the poison we drink from,
disintegrating our joy,
caping possibility.
the antithesis of love.
yet our choice still remains,
the power to renounce
all thereof.

the flame of our passion begins to lick at the air.
as articles of clothing are left abandoned.
where my mind should be enthralled in this erotic scene,
gets interrupted by the faint voice of treason:
"you will lose it again."

there.
planted.
is the seed of my downfall.
the one that recalls a different occasion
one in which my body deceived me,
stillness where i pressed for excitement.
disappointment impeding.

as one seed germinates,
so do a million more
as my mind spins in circles,
losing connection, i fall.
softly.

reading my lover's face,
is it annoyance or frustration?
i'm unable to converse.

her hand finds my chest as she pushes me to the wall.
a mischievous smile creeps over
as she proceeds to take control
where my perception of being broken,
pressure to perform
fear of inadequacy
is shattered once + for all.

self reflections:

1. what are my internal critical thoughts about myself or my partner in sex?
2. where/who did these beliefs come from?
3. how do they get in the way of my own connection to pleasure?
4. what are my feelings about these critical thoughts? take these statements + write a more preferable, empowering narrative. use them as counter argument anytime these old stories arise.
5. have i ever shared about these stories to a lover before? vulnerability can be a powerful aphrodisiac when shared with a partner who is safe.

on healing.

the essence of his touch.
i shutter in the remembering.
cold.
hard.
greedy.
invading.
misattribution,
as my lover takes me on.
my soul leaves my body
floating above,
detached from the experience,
and all the parts thereof.
protection that kills my delight,
replaced with indifference.
slowly poisoning my light.
to wish things were different,
i anger what he took.
my freedom, my pleasure,
he stole it,
like a crook.

patience in your touch.
presence so refined.
protection in your caring.
can't beat the demons of my mind.

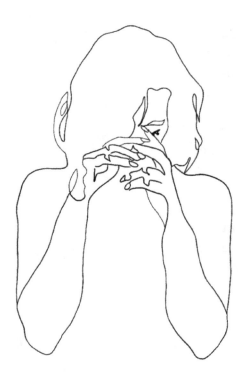

discomfort.
disconnect.
sensing.
resistance.

"we must feel it, to heal it."
but our bodies say no.

we'd rather ruminate.
analyze.
think our way through.
make up a narrative,
of connections untrue.

projections of perceptions
take residence in our head.
like a detective turning it over
and around here instead.

agonizing to be present,
to the pain that lies inside.
give me distraction from the emotion,
my tolerance is all dried.

careful not to invite in,
more awareness of the feeling.
where i may lose control
to all i'm concealing.

it's painful.
this inner work,
thing.
and the realization of my own power
that i am the creator of my own obstruction.
the thought of love to which i cower
the heart it should flow through lies overgrown, untended.
tangled with the vines
of relationships long past ended.

but you, love me, won't leave me.
be my healer + set me free.
tear down the wall
that barricades my heart.
fight your way in or else, i'll come apart.
it's easier for you to do it for me,
than to own it's my own to mend,
how far can i push you,
will you break or will you bend?

it's painful.
this inner work,
thing.
i'd rather just be cured.
but to be cured may be our parting,
as our roles no longer serve.

who would i be, without you to hold me?
complete me.
my savior to all my rash behavior.

perhaps i don't want to heal, so you'll stay longer,
the breath of you
to make me stronger.

to allow ourselves to be vulnerable is like being cracked open like an
egg. soft, smooshy, raw, + a wee bit messy,
not easily contained again as we run all across + down the counter.
funny, how we convince ourselves that we can't let go. we must
protect our innards by holding it all together. creating a shell for
protection. but it is in the cracking that we discover how good it
actually feels on the other side:
surrendered.
soft.
smooshy.
raw.
a wee bit messy.
we find it is less tiring than trying to prevent the shell from
breaking,
through efforts to lightly tread the earth
or strongly muscle our way through.

be kind.

know that your words can be like knives.
slicing my precious ego to tiny pieces.
when we are entangled,
naked + raw.
your direction can be a welcoming expression,
or shut me down with submission.

be kind.
know that your words can be my guide.
but only the type that are encouraging
when we are wrapped up,
open + loved.

self-reflections:

1. along my sexual journey, what negative sexual experiences have i had?
2. how can i see them playing a role in my current sexual expression?
3. what contextual factors about myself, my partner, or the environment would help me feel safe enough to open even a crack more?

on self as lover.

masturbation is simply sex with someone we love.

-*why do they shame?*

is it vile,
to touch my own skin?
is it selfish,
to revel my own beauty?
is it empty?
does it depreciate?
am i immoral?
when the most satisfying palpitation
resides in the trigger of my finger.

should i be sinful?
i'll commit it again.

worshipping my vessel as an idol.
banish me from this realm.
for thine structures + oppositions,
lay misery + death to the song
of inspiration.

dissonance to the idea.
for how could something so full of pleasure,
be anything that's wrong?

we forge a path to reaching our climax:
my legs must be crossed,
hips tilted
fingers dancing,
x's + o's.
slow then moving faster,
repetitive hold.
trance in building pressure.
body contracting,
breathe caught.
ecstatic pleasure,
in waves rolling through.
like that of the pacific,
my spine writhes.
fall back,
satiated.
catching back my own air.
marinating in the glow.
self-created.
head to toe.

tomorrow we do it again.
same pattern.
same flow.

yet should we embark on a new direction--
an added lover
or change in operation
we may not arrive, at the same destination.

when we fall into pattern, deciding "this is how i achieve it."
we hardwire the path.
should we instead practice expanding through conscious
attention—

incorporating changes to the play —
caressing the body,
changing the strokes,
turned onto our belly,
edging + rolls.
we create different pathways,
conditioning that pleasure need not have the same end.
while giving us a wider landscape then to roam.

seek not for a product at the end.
allowing the body to relax,
accept,
enjoy,
and be.
creating new opportunity,
for both partners + toys.
and our exquisite orgasmic pleasure,
we all can enjoy.

-my body, a beautiful instrument

romance.
a provocative word.
that artists and poets breathe life from.

how ill that we segregate it to the exchange of two lovers,
when it's essence drips like nectar
in every being,
every action,
and each unfolding.

to romance ourselves,
to romance this life,
we seek out the stunning transfiguration.
from mundanity,
we see exquisiteness,
find perfectness.
know divine.

our attitude envelops a different vibration.
reflecting care + reverence.
space + patience,
true love + held attention.
we've convinced ourselves all wrong,
and as a result of it capped our own pleasure potential.

romance needn't be from one outside another,
but a cultivated experience from deep within.

-i am my best lover.

on orgasm.

i cry out on the edge.
rolling.
tumbling.
faster.
lost.
a declaration of god's presence
followed by a momentary mute expression of rapture.

'til i crave nothing more than the sweetest release that never comes
as the edge is brought near only to make me wait + crave it more.
insanity.
to taste the tipping point that never comes.
harsh punishment i never dreamed i'd want for fun.

-edging

the pleasure rolls in.
tiny twitches.
softened moans.
pressure accumulating.
intensity shifts to high.
we can't handle it.
we can't stand it.
the desire to disconnect is strong.

yet as the eject button is about to be spoken.
a remembrance comes abound.
that this is not our capacity.
there is more to be found.

relax.
this is not the end.
just the edge.
an edge we can breathe into.
expand to hold more.
as the ecstatic wave floods our system.
leaving us higher than god himself.

"did you come yet?"
cursed words to leave thine lips.
casting foul pressure + guilt,
for one's lover to come + be done.
rather than the release that was ordered to arrive + satisfy.

our awareness crawls deep into headspace, grinding.
creating stories that we should hurry.

orgasm.
the provocative word writing love letters on our tongues.
forms for many, so different.
across each lover + each affair.
different from what's publicly presented,
creating expectations of a lie.

some are just a twitch.
while some rock the body.
some ignite energetic fire.
while some are soft and sublime.
some contain strong contraction.
while some are subtle to release.
some manifest in our tears.
while some manifest a roaring feat.

how vulnerable we are in the throes of sex + passion.
innocent questions turned around in our mind like acid.
melting the fabric of our thighs.
this peak convulsion,
is not sole evidence of satisfaction,
yet should we seek to pleasure her,
a different spell we could cast:
"tell me how your body speaks,
when she's full of ecstasy, and rising fast."

perceived destination.
our coveted end.
the more we chase after,
elusive instead.

on expanding our pleasure potential.

as children we run around free.
wiggle in our seats.
squeal loudly in excitement.
chatter with our classmates.
rub our crotch on the swing pole.
all because it just felt good.

as children we experience natural urges, feelings, needs +
we react to them accordingly.
no filter of shame or propriety.
yet often met with a command:
"stop that. sit still. don't talk. be good."

we freeze.
contract.
the program in our minds:
"to avoid punishment, i must contain."

confliction.
for what feels good, we are told is wrong.

authority figures versus the authority of our body.
body armor starts to form.
holding back emotive urges causing tightness.
over time succumbed with rigidity.

we grow older.
this ideology the main influence of our world,
caping our potential + the pleasure that can arise.
"if i let go of my restraint, then i'll be out of control."
so we tense on the sensation as it expands through our body.
sabotaging an otherwise beautiful unfolding.

-i don't want to grow up.

lust
of life.
owned by those who have learned to dance with carefree abandon,
carried through the extent of each day by the tiny pleasures of their
senses,
in the tiny moments of bodily affection.
here,
where the magnetic force of joy makes attraction.
cultivating even more satisfaction.

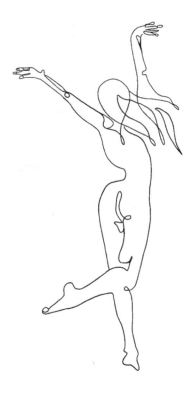

pleasure.
to some of us a filthy word.
saved for those who are selfish.
hedonistic.
irresponsible.

to sacrifice is our moral code.
to deprive ourselves exemplifies strength of the mind.
putting all others before us.
letting their needs lead us blind.

we've convinced ourselves that we are strong to withstand
disappointment.
so we withhold.
as if it's for the good of all.
honorable.
yet the days turn into years,
and our body grows in more pain.
pain from the constant tension,
restriction.
denial.
declination to what's authentic.
never permitting.
never accepting the call to want more.
we grow bored.
escaping to fantasy,
to porn,
to food,
to mourn,

the absence of all that we've dreamt
or suppressed.
observant of the carefree vagabonds,
the effervescent, the free.

how could they wear their pleasure so proudly?
like a badge glinting in the sun.
what ingredient are we missing,
that allows a casual charm?

should we bite the forbidden fruit of the garden?
or will their punishment be coming all along?

pleasure.
what a filthy word.
contaminating every atom,
electrifying every being,
sweetening every moment,
we could ever fathom.

punishment ethos
—the spirit of a culture programmed to make
decisions based on avoidance of pain,
criticism,
fear,
and anything of discomfort.
rather than motivated by what feels good.

i withdraw from you my love,
to elicit a desired response.
replacing pleasure with insecurity.
as a strategy to make you considerate of
me.
motivated by the dis-ease from potentially losing
me,
more than by the genuine desire to be with
me.

the ground you walk upon is fragile,
laden with eggshells to lightly tread.
my sensitivity for threat is high.
perception of your acts,
misred.

coming from early age conditioning,
when authorities ignored our attention-seeking.
from the belief we don't deserve the love
or that this feeling good will have an end.
unless we control
them...

unconscious to how we are keeping our lover jealous,
insecure, or guilty to get them to be more thoughtful of us.
in efforts to soothe me,

you pacify.
draining us both of our own life energy.
seeking your reaction,
impacting my enjoyment then of what is.

how complicated
to be vigilant of our actions,
maintaining specific parameters
set out
preventing ourselves
from our own authentic flow.
obstructing true intimacy,
we will never know.

-to free your soul, will pleasure into your life.

paying homage to the good flirt,
and your service unto this world.
may your light continue to shine on
as you sing to us our worth.

craving this attention.
coveted, for its nurturance.
your flirting is pure playfulness
lighting our hearts.
with your song.

sometimes rejected by the fear
that your motive here is wrong.
nervous minds fear an expectation,
of progression that might lead on.

a destination beyond this interaction,
one we don't wish to misguide,
or keep on.

this mistrust conditions our response
to believe you expect a transaction.
that you want something from our body
as your words express attraction.

our inability to receive,
as we tense up in expectation,
is not a reflection of your worth.
but two views lost in translation.

playful flirts of the world,
we need your presence here,
for your words remind us of our beauty
inspiring our inner light to appear.

it's tuesday.
i'd rather pretend it's sunday and stay in bed doing bed things.
no pressure to arrive.
arrive to nowhere,

space.
to unfold you, just to fold you.
the sweetest origami, i love to woo.

sex. expanded

oftentimes in our culture, sex exists as a taboo conversation, paradoxically juxtaposed to its simultaneous presence in our daily lives. what this has created is a culture of confusion, contributing to challenges in our sexual functioning, creating shame + preventing us from being able to express + talk openly about it. as more conversations are finally rising out of the ashes of our shame-riddled history + proper education is replacing free + fantastical pornography, we are peeling back the layers of shame left by our protestant ancestors to reveal an opportunity for freedom + authentic connection. rewriting the internal beliefs that are not our own, yet have been ruling our behaviors for millenia, we come into an era of greater empowerment + enjoyment.

what we identify as "sex" illustrates itself upon our minds almost like a script, comprised of everything we've experienced in our lives-- and it heavily impacts our eroticsm. what we receive from the media, culture, + our own family of origin shapes our brain in such a way that it affects our response to the various cues that either increase or inhibit arousal. these messages also determine the meaning + expectations we have surrounding relationship, sex, + intimacy. for example, pornography has been a major topic of controversy concerning its affect on the cultural + personal schema of sex.

many activists complain that pornography is a violent or unrealistic portrayal of day-to-day sexual activity. scenes are often filmed using the best lighting, the perfect angles, + fantastical storylines such as sex with the plumber, the pool boy, the babysitter or other unusual pairings that would not typically occur in real life. further, pornography is filmed with the intention of being sensational + entertaining + does not accurately represent the natural progression of our needs for arousal. scripted scenes demonstate lube-free anal sex, little to no foreplay before pentration, men easily getting erect without touch, + then culminate in over-the-top simultaneous orgasms.

due to the lack of accurate, pleasure-focused education + the easily accessible pornographic material online, it has become the primary source of learning what "sex" looks like for much of our culture's present day youth + adults. If we forget that the intention of porn is for entertainment + not education, then these images we see on film become the reference point to which we compare our actual experiences of sex. ss a result we can feel a sense of inadequacy, unfulfillment, + harbor unrealistic impressions of what we should be doing to acheive a satisfying sex life. typically, we are not aware of this script running in the background until our expectations or needs are significantly unfulfilled, eventually leading to a critical point in our ability to cope. we then have the opportunity to question these underlying meanings + make the most beneficial changes possible, causing a full circle return to an authentic self-connection.

as partners, we can fall in the trap of seeing our significant other as an extension of ourselves, assuming our partner's sexual desires + needs are supposed to be identical to our own. when we discover they are not, we chalk it up to incompatibility rather than taking the opportunity to learn the sexual language our partner speaks (and for our counterpart, vice versa)-- thus destroying the journey of co-creating a mutual language together. further, we are most likely in different stages of our sexual journey. some of us could be more in the healing stage, while others are in predominantly curious or adventurous stages. part of our responsibility here is to differentiate ourselves from our partner, honoring their own unique map + stage so we can get unstuck from the blame or shame of the connection lacking fluidity. sex is a natural behavior. however, pleasurable + satisfying sex is not necessarily inherent + often must be learned.

to complicate things even further, we have developed a culture that runs on a punishment ethos. we make decisions based on the avoidance of pain, criticism + discomfort.

as a result, we walk around attempting to maintain a sense of control, which causes pain, constriction + literal aches in the physical body-- from this held tension. conditioned to believe that making decisions based out of pleasure is selfish + frivolous, (a luxury even!) human beings in our society wind up sacrificing + sabotaging the ultimate success of coital relationships without even realizing it. the problem we've unknowingly created for ourselves is the impact it then has on our satisfaction in sex + our potential to feel good across life. in order to feel pleasure, we must be able to relax in the body; however, this simultaneous "letting go" can also activate fear, causing the body to tense up in an effort to regain control. therefore, it is imperative we actively practice strategies to stay relaxed + open during the building of intensity as we approach our edge-- through mindful awareness, affirmations, breathing, + leaning in. our level of tolerance for pleasure directly impacts our arousal, orgasm, sexual functioning, connection to our bodies, + satisfaction. if we stay contracted or pull away when we near the ceiling of what we've held before rather than surrendering into the feeling + trusting that we will be ok, then we can never reach a greater potential.

the antidote to this cultural issue requires us to reprogram the concepts we maintain around pleasure. we must include the consideration of "what feels good" as we make decisions based in logic. we must also learn to relax at the very start of the body's onset of contraction. we must find excitement in the expanding sensation of energy as it moves in our body. and we must learn to express what we feel + what we desire. as we do, we will notice our individual worlds soften into more enjoyment as our sexual challenges recede, their roles substantially diminished.

love.

because none of us are born knowing how to love or be loved.
until we try.
and learn.
again.

on what is love.

for what is love, save the intangible,
transcendent experience in which we recognize self again + again.
perfection in design + flawless in its orchestration.
as humans we can sometimes forget the matter,
re-writing the definition to encapsulate all our woundings, all our
fears, all our expectations for another to heal us.
complete us.
and when the words we choose to define it,
confine it,
white line it,
fail to meet the experience unfolded,
we are heartbroken.
"betrayed."
fixated on this receipt of our purchase.
pained.

i believe we forget what love is,
not because it's not everywhere + everyone,
but because it is everywhere + everyone.
hidden in plain sight.
translucent save for those who are aware.
and to those who are aware,
may we take it up as our duty to share.
as we re-narrate to remember all to what is.

what is love.
as this intangible, transcendent experience.
where we meet the self once again.

how beautiful all the world appears,
when i see it through the lens of you.

it's brave to love another.
in a world where so many feel they don't deserve it.
"you're too good for me."
"you deserve better."
"i don't want to hurt you, + i think i will."
love anyway.

it's brave to love ourselves.
in a world where so many practice a false sense of humility.
"don't brag."
"feel guilty."
"be nice…"
love anyway.

so many of us seek for love.
"where is it?"
"why don't i have it?"
"how can i get it?"
it may not be the problem that the love is not there.
overtly, we are the perfect partner,
yet covertly we block our own receiving.

contraction to a compliment.
supressing what's on our mind.
not asking for help or refusing it
staying in the relationship not for the desire to,
but for of the fear we won't be desired again.
creating distance as we closen, while wanting them to pursue.
love anyway.

it's brave to recognize love,
in a world that craves its essence + decapitates it upon arrival.

love anyway.

love exists in those quiet spaces in between.
yet we can confuse it for the rapid thrum of the hummingbird's
beat.
mislabeling anxiety for passion.
succumbing to the wear of our soul.
as it disintegrates from the inside out.

we all love to know that someone holds
a place for us to take residence in their mind.

to vortex for hours—
timeless.
with no end point or goal in mind.
to kiss the dimples of your face—
the sweetest craters of the moon.
to get lost in your ocean eyes—
drowning yet forever afloat.
this is love.

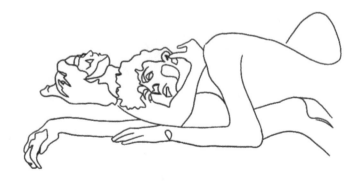

i love the way you hold your own face, as you squint at the computer to master its perplexity. i love the way your voice morphs into accents, like a room of international delights. i love the way your laugh echoes so distinctly above the crowds + across for miles. i love the way you run my jokes, long after the line of appropriateness is crossed. i love the way you make enigmatic sounds when you feel awkward + uncertain. i love the way you fall into the rhythm of my breath, so effortless in the merging.

i love the way you hold me firmly, impossible for me to leak out from your containment. i love the way you lightly brush the lashes of my eye, or kiss softly the inner corner of its crease. i love the way you dance with my body, like two beings absorbed in an alchemical trance. i love the way you say "we", as if it's the sweetest strawberry upon your tongue.

may it be apparent, i see every particle of this magnificent existence composed of the very essence that is "us."here in the quirks + little moments of awe

we fall in love, again + again. truly present to the texture of the cloth that we weave forming together the most exquisite tapestry. that tells of stories + makes up these shapes. impossible for anyone to replicate.

we do not need to earn our worth in love.
we simply are.
no need to chase.
no need to convince.
no need to convenience.
to preserve a form of love that cannot be
you.

the evidence of love does not reside in the grand gestures,
but rather the accumulation of everything that is small.
it's the acts of service when no one is looking.
love notes left on the bathroom mirror.
it's the laughter in response to little quirks.
tiny kisses that linger on the nose.
it's the knowing her sensitivities, + mindful not to hurt.
it's the patience + the presence, as tears fall to their shirt.

our mind holds a negative bias, one that scans the room for threat.
so when our fear questions the presence of love,
intentional aims in its recognition we beget.
depicting the very images of the scenes.
and as our pen scrawls across each line
we let the feelings invoked sink in.
that should the uncertainty deliver another blow.
there lies the evidence,
to mitigate the row.

why as a society do we measure the success of a relationship on length of time versus depth?
some of my greatest relationships lasted three months, two weeks, four hours, five minutes.
the three months taught me how to surrender + love my shadow.
blown so far open, i was left feeling exposed.
self-trust, my only life preserver.
learning that safety was created from within.

the two weeks taught me to soften my edges, let go, + play.
that working so much was not living.

the four hours taught me that i had a voice.
that what i wanted, felt, or feared was valid.

the five minutes was a fleeting connection in the coffee line.
lost to our own worlds, one man engaged.
a reminder that the purpose is not to avoid bumping into one another,
but rather to bump into each other.
to infect with the highest vibration of love.
to leave an imprint + move on.
unattached, but not unaffected.

all relationships are valid teachers.
if. we. let. them. be.
breaking the surface of our armor,
penetrating each layer,
melting every mask that we wear,
exposing the raw, real, human that lies underneath.
how deep we go in a minute, is entirely our own doing.

-how much can we stand, when we can no longer hide behind mere politeness?

the discourse of our love life,
as it tells a story across the seasons
can confuse our seeking hearts
breaking them for what reason?

lust seeks sexual union.
confusing it for love,
we are blind
"do i want you or just your body?"
conversations of heart + mind.

the language of romantic love,
narrows our sight to one selected mate.
"in a room full of people,
it's only you i see, my fate."

the matter of attachment,
expresses to us as companions.
where before we were two separate beings,
we now behave as one.
less thrilling,
yet crucial,
for the creation of pair bonds,
as we grow into parenthood
a shared vision of beyond.

the progression through love is natural.
witnessing the ebbs + flows along.
a slump no longer means the end.
intensity no longer means "the one."

on intimacy.

to be seen.
without trying to be fixed.
this is intimacy.

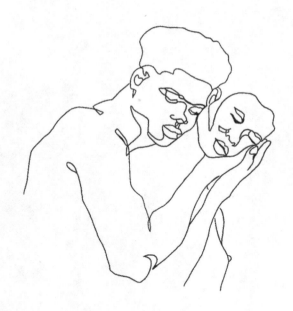

intimacy is more than sharing stories of our past,
it lies in the moment to moment contractions,
insecurities,
bids for affection + security
that are voiced— knowing that the potential for it not to be received
always lies in the space that proceeds.

how much do we allow ourselves to care?
or do we care less than the other as a means of protection?
minimizing our efforts of investment.
shrugging off the potential effects of the aftermath.
reminding the world we are evolved + unattached

we who determine the closeness + the distance.
we who determine the depth of the intimacy.
we who determine the timeline + the outcome.

is it that we do not care,
or do we not acknowledge how deeply our care actually goes?
until it is gone.
out of our hands,
yet not out of our heart.

it's brave to love.
it's brave to care.
it's brave to stay open + allow penetration of our defenses,
to feel her influence on our heart.
no assurance of safety.
no protection from harm.
yet the evidence of our resiliency is strong.
should we allow ourselves to care,
leaning into the unknown.
the greatest potential,
creating love + intimacy we can own.

there is a trap of being the savior.
for we love being able to provide.
feel needed.
but what is our true motive?
hiding behind the role?

to make us feel powerful
to give value.
to insure we have a place in their lives.
to avoid healing our own shortcomings.
yet.
staying here creates shallow intimacy,
never allowing depth for who we are.

staying here can make them our purpose in life,
distracting us from our own.

staying here can create anxiety, loneliness, disappointment,
resentment,
all the while tangled up in what we've sewn.

be nurturing.
be influencing.
be a teacher.
while allowing our own humanness to come through.
receive,
for they are our teachers, too.

true safety: when we reveal ourselves completely.

false sense of safety: when we engage in the conditioned behaviors of hiding our authentic experience. choosing to withhold our vulnerable hearts so we don't lose out on love.

- *i feel pain imagining my words make you leave.*

heart beat.
heart break.
heart beat.
heart break.
the only evidence i'm still living.
is the thrum + the crash of my heart battering.
only to rebound
in the next pulse.
where my voice carries out my truth.
that oh so raw + vulnerable truth.
leaving my insides out
for everyone to see
exposed.
naked.
tender.
my mind races through algorithms attempting to regain control.
only to fall back to a single answer of yielding.
"it's all out."

hoping for an answer that doesn't come.
yet dreaming of it still.
not yet able to recognize the power that i wield,
as my attention fixates on what's current.
the complete surrender in the knowing
there's nothing more that i can do
save the practice of patience, trust, + presence.
and enjoy the loving gaze from you.

no one is obligated to be our sole source of love + healing. yet, to prevent ourselves from the pain of loneliness, or to create protection from the chaos of the world, we might attempt to make others the proxy of what we did not get as children. conscious or not to the strategies we employ to guilt them or compel them to love us the way we think best. all the while ignoring the unique ways they already do.

in attempts to preserve the relationship with the one we perceive as the new source of our love + needs, a part inside convinces us we need to take action. we need to regain control.

what happens if we instead choose to allow?

dropping the need to do anything, say anything, or be anything other than what's authentic + alive.

some of us err on the far side of caution + protection— pulling away to prevent the anticipated hurt.

some of us err on the far side of connection— latching onto another to be the source of love + calm.

as we oscillate between these two poles, can we find awareness in our visceral state, have compassion for our emotional state, become curious by our mental state, + identify where we fear. the barrier to love coming into place.

on insecurity.

we seek to be special,
the only one that will do.
as a result we get frantic,
sabotaging what they view.

-you don't know me.

the years of our youth leave imprints of how we see.
creating an image of love, of trust + dependency.

tainted are our proceeding relationships.
we are vigilent to prove:
"i am not wanted; i am bad; i am unsafe."
ignoring or avoiding anything that would argue
as if to prevent the clues that it's untrue.

what we deem as "evidence"
as it infiltrates our perceptions,
activating our senses.
influencing our mind, our feelings, + our actions.

we expect all others to leave us,
unaware of our own contribution.
as they stop pursuing, we are validated:
"i am unloved."
casting our lovers + friends as the main characters of our story.
convinced they see us as the same flawed self that we do.
surprised when they keep showing up.
not surprised when they don't.
"see?"
in those moments our system activates
perceiving a threat to our own connection.

we forget,
that they, too, have their own fears + insecurities.
mutually feeding + activating,

blind, as we grip tightly to our story.
inhibiting the potential for true intimacy to emerge.
until we wake up from the illusion of our faulty beliefs
that suggest we do not deserve.

jealousy + it's palpable impression.
as it drips like poison
from the eyes of her expression.

fear-laced + powerful
birthed in response to his action.
flaring up as a threat
causing our retraction.

common to human nature
yet we deny that we feel it.
suppressing the rising wave
as if we can't emit it.

painful--
the perception
of violation to what is ours.
activation--
of our defenses
through aggression
we lose our powers.
conditioned to believe,
it's undesirable to possess.
yet it rages on internally
beneath the surface--
of our chest.

convinced we cannot be loved
amid this ugly human mess.
"i am fine."--the words repeated.
a wall containing all the stress.
as it drains the waters of intimacy dry.
never trusting + never showing
our own truth beneath the lie.

the tests we set to see how much they love us,
quite often is not our intention.
we wait + we watch.
"will you pick me above them all?"
their body speaks of their decision.
and to that, our face falls.
their choice in opposition to what we held as our vision.
our eyes plead with a look of confusion,
"what's wrong with me?"
our repetative delusion.

we all want to feel in our hearts we are chosen.
amid every flaw + human imperfection.
that across all circumstance + over any other,
it is still us that they choose
to have this romance.
that we are not just some happenstance.

with the placement of these tests,
we are attempting control.
our body contracts,
as if to protect our own soul.
an undercurrent of pressure
weight bearing down,
we unconsciously respond
by our actions to shutdown.

if instead we expressed what it is we feel,
giving guidance to our love,
all that's vulnerable + real.
we empower through agency
instead of manipulating through fear.
knowing it took no trick or game,
to get them to be here.

what do we mean when we say we are 'not enough?'

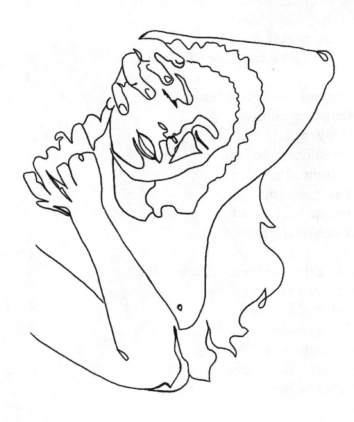

do we ask for love?
or do we turn it down when it's offered,
believing it's tainted,
not right,
or can't be trusted.

self-reflections:

1. do i find that i can speak authentically for what i feel or need?
2. how do i stay connected to my emotions or my needs as they come alive?
3. am i present to the fluctuating emotional states or needs of my partner or do I stay isolated in my own protection or resentment?
4. what do i know about my own vulnerabilities or negative self stories from my youth?
5. am i aware of these vulnerabilities of my partner?

on stories.

when we don't have all the details,
our mind writes stories + calls them fact.
we process in our heads,
their perspective we detract
the bias of the mind, not always helpful, nor whole.
influenced by our past, a challenge to patrol.

to truly listen, we find our presence
letting their experience settle in our bones
feeling their hearts + the sense we can gather
that makes their story seem as fair as our own.

reflection of what we hear them say
for our perception may not be the words that they relay.
missing something in their expression
or those key words
inevitable digression.

to slow ourselves down,
participation in attention.
open + curious
seeking clarity through each question.

they are in support of us
not intentional harm of us.
though their words are profane + harsh
they are in protection
or projection
of inner wounds that lead the march.

careful we must be of our own stories
where we can mix up fact + fiction
outdated ideas that impact the script we speak from
causing our affliction.

a starfish is a fragile creature,
only protected by the thin incasing shell.
how intricate the design
of this hard protective layer.
how detailed we can become,
the words of our story,
to prevent us from impending harm.

even though we are constructed of fragile material,
it does not mean that we cannot weather a storm fully exposed
throwing out the old stories, the masks, the white lies that cover.
to stand tall + fully raw.
unapologetic, + nude.
we will discover our resilience
imbued.

why do we keep returning to the past in order to sit in the stories,
the emotions, the heartbreak that resides there?
we chew + we chew.
cud in our mouth.
tough + unbreakable.
somehow captivating.
familiar.

do we actually find what it is we seek?
taking residence amid the past pain + wounded narrative?

identifying:
"this old role,
this old feeling
this old belief:
the truth of my being."
preventing us from seeing who it is we have become,
since then.
our growth, our skills, our new understandings.

we go back + affirm:
"i was not wanted."
applying the old script to today:
"i am not wanted."
negating this evolution,
all the work we have mustered.
preventing us from pursuing
any new evidence that'd suggest the counter.

to dip into the past, only to bring forth the wisdom
taken from each circumstance.
is to find that sweet spot to help rather than hinder.
learning when it is right
to spit out, swallow, or surrender.

white + black.
the type of thinking that will hinder relationships.
yet attractive for its false sense of certainty.
this or that.
that or this.
yet life is not so certain,
nor is there one reality for us all.
no one owns the truth
yet our belief creates a brawl.

dialectical thinking:
where two seemingly opposite ideas co-exist,
the point at which multiple realities are actualized,
and absolutes cannot persist.
it is here, we find greater freedom.
holding that our partner is both considerate + absent minded,
unhealthy + beneficial for our growth.
we can hold that someone perpetrating tough love can be callous +
compassionate.

multiple feelings can live in the same moment.
reprieve from the always, the never, the everything,
as we relax our definitive grip,
seeing conflict all so wholey, flexible,
more feasible to work with.
internally + externally,
we find our peace of it,
herewith.

on communication.

we pursue.
he pulls away.
we want to clear the air.
he feels crowded, needing space.
triggered by the distance,
we reach out for connection.
"see me."
"hear me."
"be available to me."
but he only glances over our way,
choosing not to feel us--
or lacking the ability to.

he protects,
not feeling himself to be seen.
the friction of missed connection coming across as harsh + mean

communication--an impressive dance of habit.
guided by the reactions of our partner's step.
the response to the response,
as we whirl around the room.
sometimes our steps, in competition.
both trying to lead + trip up in doom.

no one was the start of this dance.
as no one can be blamed for its continuance.
everyone is a part of,
and unwittingly reinforcing.

the response to the response.
a par for the course.
'til both can unite in patience + presence
to feel the gentle moving force.

take a breath.
after her words meet your ears.
before your words leave your lips.
that space in between exchanges,
the medicine you need to curtail unintended reactions;
to reduce unconscious harm;
to receive what was said;
to gather your thoughts;
to relax your tension.
to drop the projection,
and prevent the fall to pattern.

take a breath.
pause.
letting the space in between bring you power.

silence sounds loudly in comparison to our words.
creating vast oceans between us + our lover.
a heavy void in separating coasts,
onto which we project with uncertainty:
"are you mad?"
"is something wrong?"
"do you still see me?"
"do you want to be with me?"
"am i enough?"

as the spiral of narration extends across pages.
while the unspoken origin exists on far off land:
"he should already know what's wrong."
"i feel so alone."
"i just want more space."
"i'm afraid to tell him how i feel."

as the shore grows more distant.
sometimes we are conscious to these words we hold within
or invent that they are something else.
sometimes we are frozen to speak for fear of what may ensue.
disconnection to escape the present discomfort.
and yet.
the "safety" we find here, amid the heaviness of our silence,
only perpetuates the distance.
the feeling alone.
the misunderstanding.

but what if instead we reach across that ocean?
to be vulnerable + truly seen.
"if i'm feeling this confusion + aloneness, maybe they are, too?"

we could make connection.
where communication + love can flow through.

on injury to love.

it was half past eight,
seared in my memory that date.
having made her descent,
the sun had long passed.
left the room that i sat in, darkness so vast.
save the glow of the small screen,
a source of life that i clinged.

as i consumed each word
upon each page
upon each email there written.
each text chain delivered.
each photograph sent in.
like a car crash embedded on the side of the road,
my eyes could not break from the tragedy to unfold.
for each word i took in that passed breathless by my lips
was a straight stab to my heart.

what a careless infringement.
and the most fascinating part,
rested in the now surreal understanding,
that every fantastical belief I had held about love.
about life.
about memory.
jaded.
as much as i wanted,
i was not his only one.

one.
a number once special,
now elaborately undone.
where the evidence witnessed should wreck violence to my limbs,
i silently sit numb in endless contemplation.

fascination with the cruelty.
yet confused all the same
how could i be so clueless, so stupid?
my thoughts fill with shame.
to have not voiced the questions that plagued?
to have allowed for the space that he begged?
to have trusted when all else seemed to counter,
leaving me questioning my own mate.

as i make the first break
staring off into the void.
my only comfort lies in the truth that I hold.
this tear of the veilance.
this break of the old.
is only the beginning,
if i might be so bold.

gaslighting.
experienced by our senses + taken note in our mind.
we share our understanding, our feeling,
only to be met with how we were wrong.

"you believe I would do that to you?"
"you don't know what you're talking about."

the dissonance we take on.
confusion for what to believe.

the self-respect + worth we hold,
directly influences our degree of doubt.
when we don't have the skills to self-inquire,
or have the trust in our mind + heart.
when we seek others to interpret our reality,
or surpass the threshold of what we can tolerate,
we are susceptible to this hurt.

like the image of fog blanketing a gaslit street—
where everything laid out there is blurry,
shadow figures may not be what they seem.
while in this state of confusion, we can't decipher what to keep.
the poison runs fast, deadly to those who wait.
unless the antidote is received + consumed straight away,
the victim shall wither 'neath this disorienting fate.

mindfulness—to recognize one's internal process.
self-care—to reduce vulnerability to fatigue.
self-love—to strengthen our own trust + validation.
self-respect—to know when to leave.

like prescription glasses to redefine the blur,
we need not fear the potential of being alone.

the state of shame absorbs us into our own sense of self + wrong
being—
preventing us from truly being able to hold the experience of the
other.

it isn't until we can embody the guilt—
the empathic, relating, embodied experience of her—
inspired by the hurt we have caused,
can we begin the process of healing.

that time i asked to come over + you wanted more space + time.
i undo you.
that time i needed you to stay + you told me i'd be just fine.
i undo you.
that time i suspended my own mind,
to favor what i knew you wanted.
i undo you.
that time you brushed me off, like lint on your sleeve.
that time i still gave you my heart so naive.
that time you told me i needed to be softer.
for my intensity to be more subdued.
that time you told me i had too much control.
that my stress was not welcome by you.
i undo you.

in the aftermath the clarity can reveal.
your rejection of self was needed to be worked through,
while the discomfort of the work, for you was unbearable.
thus the projection onto another.
me.
to hold the work of a mirror.
to see,
all that which you do not like in another was nothing to do with my
worth.

yet, i held it + owned it.
how unwilling i was to let you feel your own pain.
i undo you.
not because i don't care, but what is not mine is not mine.
the imprinted memories + the spirit of that time,
i give back for you to hold.
my gift.
that we both find greater freedom,
beyond this painful narrative that we told.

when we experience betrayal (whether that be through a discovered affair, or the mere breaking of the expectations we had of who we thought they should be), it can impact us like a traumatic event. our brain + nervous system respond to the recognition of threat in our environment. no longer are we in the rational frontal cortex of the mind, but rather we shift to the limbic system and operate as if in survival mode.

through this lens we respond in a myriad of ways, invoking our strategies for protection. perhaps we displace the pain onto something else or we deny that it has happened at all. perhaps we become fixated on the smallest of details in order to conceal the more distressing emotional pain, thus making the experience more tolerable. perhaps we rage in blame + victimization, casting one character worse than our own name. perhaps we own the reality, yet lie to the rest of the world to save face + preserve what can be perceived by others. perhaps we numb it out altogether, in hopes that it will all soon be over.

what's more than the pain of the act itself is often the confusion that can ensue as a result of the dissonance. we clench onto a belief that "he is not that type of guy" or that "she will never hurt me" + grapple with a reality that does not fit.

here we are more susceptible to gaslighting by the efforts to confuse us or expressions of denial, a disposal of inconsistencies that threaten the structure of our lives. to preserve our own attachments, our own belief systems, our own false sense of safety, we will travel many lengths. along the way, silencing the internal process + maiming our sense of self-trust. perhaps we meet the day that the lies we've told can't hold us here + we are left to make a decision. a decision that asks us, do we stay or do we leave? this question is not one to be made rash, but rather one to be given space to breathe + thought through, as we invite our collective parts to speak, shining light on the patterns, the stories, + our body's primary state. what happens when the world finally cracks + we are left with nothing in the aftermath? viktor frankl writes in *man's search for meaning* (2), "everything can be taken from a man but one thing: the last of the human freedoms--to choose one's attitude in any given set of circumstances, to choose one's own way."

so my darling, perhaps the breakdown can by chance be your breakthrough. the one you did not even know you needed.

on resentment.

betrayal.
the breaking of the expectation we held of this person.
a major break.
smaller disappointments.
lack of reliability.
or the realization of difference.

it hurts.
yet, it's not the act of betrayal that causes the most damage,
but the poor way we navigate it thereafter.

self-righteousness.
impatience.
lack of compassion in the other.
the overtaking of anger,
shaming ourselves rather.

hard focus on what's "broken"
as we forget all that's good--
the glue for re-building
the establishment of trust.
we take time in the healing,
while making movement to adjust.

resentment.
the heavy residue left in our bodies after an emotional injury.
thick.
sticky.
suffocating.
tightly gripped, as if the source of our own power.
a false sense of authority.
one we become fools to.
believing that by vocalization, we get support, attention, or their validation.
believing it's not our obligation, leaving them the work of navigation
believing the hurt will burn them as we hold the anger in our heart alone.

yet it is *we* who are stuck with the thick, heavy, contention.
waiting for anything else to come along.
the antidote of forgiveness tastes bitter,
that first drop upon the tongue,
growing sweeter as it sits.
loving kindness to go along.

upon another soul, we wouldn't wish it.
seeing them as human,
still evolving like our own.
sending well wishes—
relaxing our hard scold.
setting better boundaries.
choosing ourselves to powerfully uphold.

i need you to have feeling words so i can be close to you.
i need you to have intuitive eyes so my pain can be understood.
i need you to have sensitive ears so my story can be heard.
i need you to have unwavering foundation so i can step soundly
i need you to have a place for me in your mind so i can be a part of
every decision.
i need you to have endless patience so i can make all of my mistakes.

we ask for our needs to be met by another,
becoming resentful when they are not.

frustration: the space between points,
where we are + where we want to be.
stuck in a stalemate.
two people,
two lives,
the difference in our realities.
yet the desire's all the same.

we want to be seen.
we want to be loved.
so relentless we protect our position.

her needs are real yet unspoken,
our needs are real + are vocal.
knowing the limits in our own expression,
can help us shift our own expectation.

seeking connection through empathy
realizing the truth:
we are two
instead of one.
meeting her here,
as just a human.

the letters fell out from your lips
like black tea dripping down the side of the cup:
loose.
watery.
staining the table upon which it sat.
"i'm sorry."
strange, for i couldn't grasp at the point of the expression.
"i'm sorry."
for your face + your body told me a different story.
"i'm sorry."
i felt the texture of my response as it slipped out in automation.
split-minded confusion.
meaningless disillusion.
where we both pretend that our words indicated something,
knowing it was all formality.
weaving lies as if to comfort our wounded hearts.
preferring the false pretense
over the reality
that would make us wrong.

never have we wasted a single moment of our lives.
every relationship that ended,
or gone on too long.

every moment we spent.
frozen between prospects.
every kiss that felt off,
every afternoon spent lazy,
every "wrong" decision, that made us feel crazy.

we give credit to our evolution.
a compilation of what we have seen.
space holders + all.

these experiences are the correct ones,
as they continue to unfold.
no wasted time.
only lessons that go unnoticed.

on trust.

bodies + the shapes we make in trust.
trust.
we believe we grasp at the meaning,
yet fail at the true comprehension.
we speak the words.
yet our body holds a separate conversation.
one in which we may not be a part of.

contraction when she touches.
tension when they take the lead.
rigid from fear for unrequited expectation.
stiff to maintain certainty.
stress to ensure our security.
blocking our own reception of joy.
getting caught on the past,
preventing pleasure in the now,
fulfilling of our own prophecy.
a possible break after all.

instead,
toward the contracting sensation, we breathe.
settling the nerves.
unclenching the jaw.
grounding into our skin.
surrendering to love
to lead us therein.

the sound of trust breaking.
like a heavy anvil to the pavement.
we feel the sadness, the shock, the isolation, the betrayal.
our world disoriented.
where nothing here makes sense.
we try to stabilize, yet the horizon is off kilter.
in attempts to rebuild, where do we go?

to choose feeling safe over deeper intimacy:
yelling profanity,
blaming insanity.
seething hatred from our pores.

to choose appearing more powerful over human vulnerability.
threatening attack,
intention to scare,
to prevent another betrayal.

in truth we believe that it helps
until the realization concedes:
that setting fire to the space of comfort set in their arms
provides us that desired safety
but finds that we are alone.

when trust is broken, we lean into risk again + again, in order to develop the new evidence that it can hold us. should we keep the wall up, weary of the injury to reoccur, we sabotage its potential + can be left with injury. mind you, rebuilding trust is a process. one in which we are exposed + vulnerable, misattributing occasions as their carelessness towards us once again. as we replace the old script of pain with a new one. it's not that we don't establish boundaries, or that we are perfect at acceptance. but when the wall rises up, we vocalize its presence. "here i am. observing this process of trust. while still i can see that my fear resurrects a wall between us."--the act of taking down the wall, as we verbally acknowledge the vulnerable truth that we still fear amid the desire that we don't. accepting ourselves in the exact process we find ourselves. letting another see our flaws.

remembering how we fell into love
can help us discover the path back to it,
when we've tripped on stones only to lose our own way.

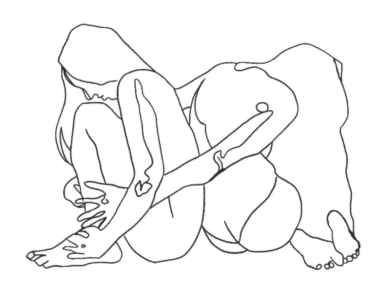

now i allow the greatest to take over, + i surrender my whole being
to that.
i exhale mistrust + doubt, as i inhale my highest excitement.
i am at peace knowing it is all unfolding just as it should.
i cannot make a wrong decision.
even if i could.

today, may we relax even the subtle contractions we hold
today, may we create allowance.
today, may we remember what we imagine is not nearly as
magnificent as what we have not experienced just yet.
today, may we stay open.
today we transmute + heal.

on shadows.

into the darkness we go.
where all the shadows of who we are take residence.
the parts of us we deem unfit.
unloveable.
unkept.

we start our descent,
uncertain of where it ends.
as we plunge deeper into the caves,
the pressure of the air increases.
the buzz of discomfort in our bones.
deafening is the sound of silence.
echoing louder with each zone.

we pause.
the furthest reaches of our heart,
to whisper softly into the void:
"i love this part, too."

we begin the process of reclamation,
to every part of us that's due.
as ours.
as love.
into wholeness.
into view.

a sigh escapes our lungs.
a settling in our bone ensues.
a heaviness is lifted.
we begin our journey to ascend.
we-emerging into the light
where we can see ourselves,
be ourselves,
own ourselves into new existence.

to see these shadows, not as separate, unique entities,
but as a collective human experience,
to love them each + every time they surface,
is the antidote to every block of our intimate existence.

we don't have to let them rule our lives.
we don't have to let them run amok.
for once we show them awareness, attention, compassion,
they calm.
no longer being resisted or rejected.
allowing ourselves to be whole.

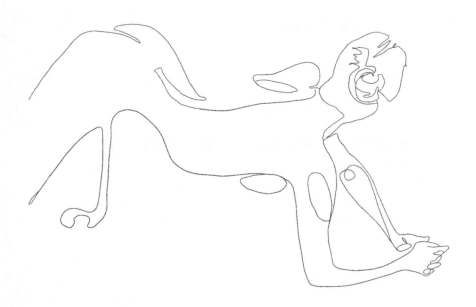

here i am, vulnerable + raw.
owning that i fucked up.
and through my lineage I can see the pattern,
veins running red + deep.
these relationships i've called in to replay
the unconscious wounding,
i cast the main characters again.
unaware of my attempts to correct what once was missing.
so easy to blame another for their ill-equipped ways of love,
than to hold + own my own part.

so here i am,
vulnerable + raw.
projecting you meet me here.
in the depths of insight + undersatnding.
wanting to see that you own your own flaws, too.

but instead i hear a lecture.

and in response to that i retreat.
resigned.
a faux smile on my face.
a false sense of peace to preserve us.
ashamed to vocalize the pain that I feel.

what i had hoped would spring a moment of closeness,
crumbles my heart
i'm all alone.

we want to test the strength of the chair under pressure
before we commit to sitting ourselves down.
yet if we keep to the incessant testing,
we may find that we break it sooner.

what is the process of working with and healing our shadow?
the parts of us we do not like,
thus hide in a bag + lug around.
heavy on our shoulders.

we think the solution is to separate.
but in reality, is to integrate.

conscious awareness—
that we may see it as it occurs.
acknowledgement—
that we may halt it by calling attention.
compassion—
that we may grasp our mere humanness.
acceptance—
that we may love ourselves as we are.
transmutation—
that we may see in it the medicine.
integration—
that we may apply it in times that aid.
repeat—
as we strengthen new conditioning.

aggression isn't appropriate at times,
yet, in others, can save our lives.

the mode of operation for becoming whole + healing.
a practice tried again after again.
as we satisfy each turn that's wheeling.

on choosing ourselves
powerfully.

these internal battles,
fought over and over by the need to prove enough.

our poor nervous system.
shot out because "she could not keep up."
buzzing as hard as she was able.

our poor heart.
broken because she could not keep open.
consumed with trying to hold it together.

our poor mind.
exhausted because she could not stay focused.
processing as quick + as much as she was able.

our poor body.
limp from lack of rest.
racing on fumes, pushing past all the signals.

what would we experience should we step back from the game?
to allow that slower, kinder, solid pace.
where once we fought hard to make it all work.
we now settle like ashes, light upon the earth.

what would we experience should we love ourselves anyway?
allowing the narrative of enoughness to be written
where once our own measure was determined by the other. replaced
by ourselves, as our own best lover.

we live our lives in cycles.
shifting like the moon.
we ebb + we flow.
we wax + we wane.
at times flowing with exuberance.
followed by trickles of a stream.

we can deny this natural movement,
deciding to press on through the ebb
to favor the flow.
in brute force we go.
'til we find ourselves hitting resistance.
heaviness taking over.
as our bodies plead for us to slow.
we surrender.

a reminder of the moon,
who, too, retires
'fore she can shine again in brightness.

the former self—cringing at the thought of how we once were.
the one we have pity for.
who felt powerless,
afraid.
the one we don't want to claim was us.
denying, shaming, blaming that being--
can only cap the potential we would grow into.
their heart could only know so much,
doing the best with what they had.

may we own our own power, choosing how we move forward.
trusting our future selves do the same.
ho'oponopono.

it is not an act of betrayal to our past self,
should we decide to let it go.

i release the grip to the fears of loss, less, + never.
fear of losing you.
fear of less time with you.
fear of less attention from you.
fear of never having you look at me in that special way again.
that i may speak, act, be in what's authentic,
trusting the outcome,
trusting you.
the unease may return in waves,
as visceral guests to my house some days.
when i witness them arise
my commitment to release them.
holding myself,
i thrive.

the mighty river flows with such great power, penetrating the earth
+ carving its course through the land without a conscious thought
of how it tears.

to harness this power, we've intentionally set dams, creating
channels to direct its movement.
to benefit our land with specific intention.
intention to life, renewable energy, food, land.
is it wrong to set these boundaries + disrupt what is natural?

boundaries set clearly + with intention
written like manuals instructing how to love us.
conscious not to pollute the waters,
that life may continue to team from within them.

on the end of a love.

the sound of your kisses on my shoulder, minutes after you call out
the end.
the sound of my heart shattering, moments after i allow the feelings
to set in.

the sound of our tears hitting our shirts.
i want to push you away, the source of the pain.
i want to pull you in, the source of my comfort.

i anger.
i love you.
i want you.
i want out.

to shut my eyes or look away.
to see your face only brings me pain.
your eyes like glass through the welling of tears,
cleansing, absolving you from the accountability of harm.

my heart beats.
my blood pumps.
my will feels weak.
my tongue so heavy.
powerless to respond.
frozen in this moment so long.

it grew stale—
this vapid love.
thing.
we didn't know how to revive.
staring into the face of us involuntary roommates.
agreed.

not seen.
not desired.
not inspired.
cherished,
yet not charged.
there.
still.
unmoving.
growing old.

what do we do when our lives have so intertwined?
what do we say when the most buzz we feel is that of our electric
toothbrush?

what do we think when our identities are enmeshed + the world
only knows us as,
us?

so far away, yet breathing distance apart.
we feel each other's presence.
the start of this trail + the end.
neither of us can move,
captivated by the one we called our lover.
still love.
and we are simply left with the only moving forward we can come
up with.
the fissure cracks til the bone does break.

the decision was made.
the break did happen.
by the very act, our lover is choosing to live a life without us.
without us.
the truth can hit hard.
devastating to our system.
the system that ran on the energy input of two,
now working in overdrive to cover with one.

the readjustment.
the phantom limb.
feeling their form, even though they aren't there.
the future, the plans, the quests that began
are all but a glimmer.
gone.

from the envisioned potential to the silence of death.
we grieve or we hold on.
we allow or we wallow.
we surrender or we chew.

rumination but a terrible habit.
"if i solve the mystery of why it all ended..."
yet our mind could never create as grand a story as the truth.
not by the first draft + not by the twelfth.

the reality remains:
we are not together.
and a life was chosen,
to be lived here without us.

tough love.
on a tough heart.
reminding us of how resilient we are.

amid the pain,
the "fuck you"-s.
the tears + the fears.
we survived + we still live.

we feel in order to heal.
however long our heart does take.
declaring we shall never leave our own side again.
growing stronger with each passing moment,
living a life in love with ourselves herein.

death.
to put an end to the life of a belief, a being, a relationship, an
identity.
to cut:
severing the source of sustenance feeding into such.
to let go:
allowing to wain,
wither,
decay.

we can die many times over.
to then have the chance of rebirth.
for where the stem is cut, a new head can grow back.
seeded with the resonance we prefer.

how long does the healing from heartbreak take?
as long as our little heart does want.
we can reframe.
see the value,
be grateful,
move forward.

we can find another lover,
a greater mission,
a new reality,
instant solution.

no matter.

for:
we may still dream about the loss.
wake up to the anger,
fantasize a different outcome,
bring her name up in conversation.
see her face in every stranger.

how long does the healing from heartbreak take?
as long as our feeling heart does want.
we cannot rush the restoration process.
only be accepting of ourselves amid the walk.

you occupy the depths of my mind.
wrapped
around
each
solid
structure.
folded
into
every
crevice.
a
sheer
fabric
laid
o'er
the
circumference.
seeping into every notion.
tainting every intention.
where i work to confine the oil spill
from further harming my environment,
my hands are saturated,
toxin on my skin.
oily.
black.
thick like lard.
powerless beneath the overtaking.
in heavy submission i drop my heart
as i lie awaiting its destruction.

we invest so much mental equity on those who do not reciprocate
our love.
we think that if we continue to put more love into the bank, then
our dividends will multiply.
we visualize the what if-s.
entertaining the could be-s.
hovering our thumb over the text send button.
the chance for reattachment through a response.
we fear the verbal clarity of the question:
our hope for reciprocated affection.
yet, already present lies the answer,
loud amid the silence,
in the unspoken word of the long silent sentence.
comfort will not be found here.
even if our mind still thinks it could.

if we instead took all our investments,
applying them to stock in our own selves + worth,
we may find our radiance growing even brighter;
the demand for us expanding even greater;
as our desire for any less than fades away.
should those moments of stress drive us to reach out,
again to the source of no love,
we have at least made profit in self as our leading lover,
that we can feed ourselves on then forever.

time passes.
the emotions waver.
denial.
anger.
bargaining.
depression.
acceptance...
or the egotistical indifference.
"i don't fucking care anymore."

as the emotion seeps forth from our skin.
contaminating the air around us.
a most powerful "indifference."
coloring our past love story with a tint of red.
the sweet words she spoke were but a lie.
the gifts he gave were but a manipulation.
the time we spent was but an obligation.
the love we made was but a good token.
we think we are "letting go" by imagining these things.
we think we are moving on by viewing it so bleak.
we think we are empowering our self worth,
owning that we are better than.
but the poison only causes more pain.
more separation.
more victim.
more shame.

the end.
but the story isn't closed.
or at least not in the language we prefer.
so we chase it.
"write the ending that you hate to see me go, but it's for the best."
"write the ending that doesn't really end but instead picks up in a new chapter."
poke. push.
text. call.
see me. tell me.
show me. pick me.
on + on + on it goes.
draining our reserves + leaving us on empty.
distracted by the story,
blinded by the object,
we miss the point all together,
perhaps we don't need the closure, tie, or conversation.
in hopes for more information,
the "right" information,
to settle down our soul.

we project they can touch that place within--
the internal understanding,
the spirit of their truth.
yet that projection may be our own lie invented,
to protect ourselves from the ultimate reality,
the choice to live a life without us.
nothing more.
it's just our own war.
decapitating our hearts from within.

is it true that i miss you,
or is it the feeling of having you as "mine"
that i ache?

we make a declaration to the self.
channeling our love back to us.
choosing ourselves most powerfully.
as thoughts of longing for the other,
are directed back to our own body.

i am my own beloved.
i am the one of my dreams.

on healing.

we unknowingly tie our self-worth to the end of how another has
made us feel.
like a kite in the wind, we get caught,
taken high,
soaring.
strong.
only to dive fast straight down at any quick shift of the breeze.
and of course.
because we are looking for evidence to influence our reality.
the knowing of who we are in the world.
yet the truth of the matter,
as hard as it may seem:
we are more than what they decided of us.
a rather complex array of color on canvas,
if we can only remember now what that palate comprised.

they said that someday i would forget your name,
but when no one was looking,
i had swallowed you whole
so you could swim in the veins of my bloodstream,
and i could live off of the sustenance of every memory about you.
every message i had ever kept.
every song + every poem i had ever written about you.
addiction to the emotion
that kept me warm with recognition,
while heavily weighing on my heart.

they said that someday i would forget your name,
but when no one was looking,
you had become so deeply ingrained
that to forget you,
i would have to forget myself.

the tear in the fabric.
our hem goes undone.
we pull it to close it,
unravels it does.
how precious was our cover,
now piles of thread where we lay.
worthless.
imperfect.
tired.
dismay.

i hate you couldn't hold me.
i hate that you strayed.
i hate that you told me,
"my heart's here to stay."

so I pick up the yardage,
untangling each strand.
fully present with each pick-at,
aware of each pain.

pain in the knots,
that every string decided to hold.
mending my heartache,
reclaiming my soul.

as each thread turns back into fabric,
as every fabric into a robe.
a new set of covering
to protect from the cold.
i step forth a new figure,
all brightened + gold.

it can be hard to receive it.
this medicine they hold.
it's painful.
cold.
relentless.
yet gold.

i hate that i choose this.
this avenue to grow.
through the contracts i made,
with every conspiring soul.
learning forgiveness.
learning compassion.
learning to let go.
learning to love.

learning acceptance.
learning my power,
learning my resistance.
learning to be free of.

penicillin holds the poison,
in the dosage,
of this mold.
yet with the reaction,
the discomfort,
and in timing,
the healing does hold.

as long as we're willing,
as long as we're looking.
we can find it.
we can see it.
all of it + its role.

"i forgive you…"
for not knowing how to love + let love in.
for choosing to be right over seeing me in my fear.
for projecting doubt + mistrust.
for ignoring my tear.
for attacking with words you knew would hit wounds.
for choosing to anger, leaving me alone + misunderstood.
for shutting down conversations,
in place of seeking out connection.
for reverting back to patterns that only made sense when you were
thirteen.
for not being able to speak the words that would have made you
feel seen.
for placing your pain onto me, testing for the "inevitable end."
for not knowing how to love + let love bring you back in.

"i forgive me…"
for all i do is the same.
blocking our own shots at love here.
an exquisite dance of pain.
as i'm truly understanding, on my cellular level, now.
how we all seem to be doing, the best that we know how.
seeking love.
seeking to be seen.
to be heard, held, + chosen.

we must make a hard choice,
one that requires our own voice.
taking the first step towards love.
to reach out + understand with compassion.
the first step towards connection
even if it's always started by me
choosing love over protection.
oh what more could we be?

if love were a mirror, + our partner, our reflection
to the exact point we are in our own evolution.
to see the image held for us, recognizing it as self.
seeing the scar instead of a flaw,
as our own wounding showing up in our other.
to hear the narrative of our minds criticizing, shaming,
as the monologue of our own self-degradation;

here lies our greatest teacher on compassion.
but only if we choose it over fear.
relationships end.
not because someone is terrible,
but because we have forgotten to show love for our self.
or maybe it's that we have grown in our capacity to hold ourselves,
no longer matching the ability of our lover.

if love were a mirror, would we allow our pupils to swell
taking in all the light that we see,
or does our body shudder before the image that's reflected.
cringing 'neath the knowing of our possession.

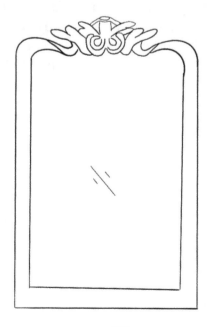

the path of healing is a process which takes time to find relief. during injury to love, our identities (who we are and how we've lived), may be shattered, leaving us with pieces that we try to put back together and make sense of. who are we in this new role, without the other?

it's imperative that during this time we find ways to restore our own sense of self value separate from the stories we've concluded to be "true"-- about ourselves and our relationships-- given the circumstances. it is easier for us to identify with the circumstances in front of us, than it is to consider they are, in actuality, nothing about us. we are more than this experience; we are more than what happened to us; we are more than anyone else's opinion of us; we are more than what we feel. we feel rejected, yet we are not a reject. we feel a victim, yet we are not a victim. we feel powerless, yet we are not without power.

as much as we'd prefer to be in solitude, ruminating on what we did wrong or how we are wrong, it will never provide us with alleviation or the truth. instead, the resolution is found in reaching for the support systems we have, rediscovering those activities we once enjoyed doing, and learning about our excitements and opinions. we take effort to show the care for ourselves that we may have otherwise been missing. for it is only when we show up for ourselves and truly be there for what we need, are we then able to write the blueprints for everyone else to then love us, as well.

self-reflections:

1. what are some of the stories i am telling myself about myself?
2. what are some of the stories i am telling myself about my former partner?
3. what are some of the stories that i am telling myself about the relationship, breakup, + anyone else involved?
4. are these absolutely true? what supports + what refutes these?
5. how did i choose myself + my care in this relationship?
6. in what ways can i begin the reclamation of those lost parts again?

It either are some of the stories than I'm telling myself about
me? It could be ...

2. what are some of the stories I are telling myself about my
critical parent?

3. what are some of the stories that ... am telling myself about
... the relationship I'm aware of are involved?

... you were absolutely sure what supports a ... what values
... client

5. how did I chose ... ove if I am once in this relationship?

6. in what ways can I begin to deconstruct those hurt part
... mind ...

180

on loving the self.

waking to the daylight streaming in,
eyes crusted over with expired tears
of last night.
i drew my body tight in like a ball,
breath grown heavy
as it moved against the current.
seeping out through the exhaustion of my bones,
was the last bit of desire to give any more effort to the lost.
as a sigh carried with it the last remaining concern,
faint words of affection began to take over
light + careful they trickled on through.
caressing my soul like silk through my fingers.
soft + inviting.
pleasurably soothing.
sweet lyrics of compassionate love.
the practice of which is quite the art,
absent to so many who do wander.
starving for the love they believe will come from another,
perhaps never to discover the source comes from within.
blind, as we fixate on all our own failures,
all the while missing the truth:
the perfection existing in each of our hearts.
no matter the point of our odyssey,
we are.

my single wish is for you to have my eyes.
that you may see yourself the way i do,
never worrying or wondering why they couldn't stay.

when i love her,
it's as if i wear glasses
that make the whole world turn brighter.
yet when i put the same glasses on
and turn to the mirror,
what i see is clouded by all that i fear.

-needing a new prescription

layers upon layers of socially conditioned ideas
of who we think we ought to be,
overlay what lies at the root of our essence.
making it hard for us to even see.
who am i amid all that's been told?
what is the truth of my desires,
at every decision that i hold?
with each question we inquire,
removes another coat off
to retire.
'til what is left is nothing we can ignore.
naked + raw.
real + inspiring.
the self we've been coveting
along this journey transpiring.

we seek a source of love across many faces.
hoping that this is the one who comes to complete us.
and as we try on these many pairings we discover,
that the self inside is the one-true greatest lover.

care for the self is a semblance of love, yet can occur without the presence thereof.
love for the self is a practice in care, whose existence cannot be without.

you are the universe held in a single precious vessel.

self-reflections:

1. were either of us taking on the responsibility of fixing, changing, saving the other?
2. was time for self as an individual a priority in the relationship?
3. was self-development a priority in the relationship?
4. was i honoring my needs and desires in the relationship?
5. how did i express or not express these needs when they arose?
6. what did i like about who i was + how i showed up in this relationship?--qualities, feelings, actions.
7. what did i not like about who i had become in the relationship?--qualities, feelings, actions.

on freedom.

the beliefs of our fathers,
our mothers,
our culture,
forging the metal wires of the containment.
we leap around from bar to bar,
reaching outward,
pulling at the gate,
dreaming of greater lives to be lived.
'til one day the hinges of the gate collapse,
as the door falls back, wide open.
leaving entrance to the greater world that lies before.
we run to the gates' edge,
pressing, extending, our face out,
eyes drop down,
far down to the earth below.
a distance to where we had been used to.
where would it take us to step out,
to leave the confines of the cage we grew to know so well.
the cage we came to hate,
to blame,
to miserate,
now appearing all so comforting + safe.
so we settle back to the far corner of our space,
gazing intently on the open passage.
fearful for the work it would take for us to step out.
fearful for the unknowing of what could betake us.
fearful of growing old in this compromising entrapment.
fearful of never allowing ourselves to know more.
do we choose to feed the fear that holds us here?
or do we choose to feed the fear that makes us bold?
whether the belief of the can is a yes or a no.
it is so.
as our thoughts + our feelings + our actions all align,
to the outcome of construct all created with our mind.

sovereign.
i never knew the word.
as i coiled my identity around each partner like a vine to a tree,
clinging desperately to the structure + sunlight they provided.
only to dry up + wither when the tree could no longer hold me.
nourish me.
be there for me.
so i dug my roots in harder.
stronger.
hoping this would help them stay.
yet the inevitable end drew nearer.
the strength of my hold growing weaker.

alas, i had grown weary of the tree.
no longer trusting their strength
so i collapsed to the moistened earth floor,
softly held amid the bed of fallen leaves.
my tiny roots stretched out
as long as they could handle,
lapping at the nutrients of the soil.

little by little, i felt my vitality return,
color resuming,
shades of bright green where i had been burned.
as buds of blossoms began to form,
fragrant droplets glistened.

i no longer worried about who scorned.
feeling the power inside me grow larger.
the space i held expanding more.
overtime i no longer needed a tree,
i had become the tree.
finding rest + ease
nestled within the forest.

scratching at the thin encasing, that surrounds my human frame.
furious to remove the film, left by your toxic stain.
as it flakes off like snow,
to be picked up by the air,
my own skin begins to peer out,
vulnerable + bare.
arduous + consuming,
this process has got me worn,
yet every region uncovered
breathes relief as if to mourn.
while every whiff of the aspiring freedom,
is enough to incite my incessant hunger.
continuing onward—
years that i labor,
discovering new ways you ravaged my soul.
i still hold pity,
for the poor bastards who had weathered my storm.
only to become lost by the blinding blizzard.
when the day arrives that i remove that final, salty, flake,
i'll close my eyes,
make a wish,
as it's blown off my finger tip.
watching it dance through the air + off to the oblivion.
no longer a victim to your name,
i am free of you.
with full reign.

we determine now.
freedom to everyone who is closest to us.
letting them all make their mistakes,
discover their joys.
wishing them well on their journey.
recognizing that what is good for them may not come
with ease or be painless.

so we allow for their process to be theirs to hold.
simply loving them all the way through.

one eve i dreamt i was a tiny swallow,
taking flight to the sky,
that no one could follow.
free to soar high,
observing the brilliant joys outstretched before.
free to fly low,
finding depths in my sorrow.
a tiny bird with the whole world at my wing tip.
no constraints.
no direction.
just me,
in my truest expression.
oh, what it feels like to be in full liberation.
our bona fide self.
the highest elation.

on starting a new love.

opening the heart in pursuit of love.
challenging,
to begin the journey all over
again.

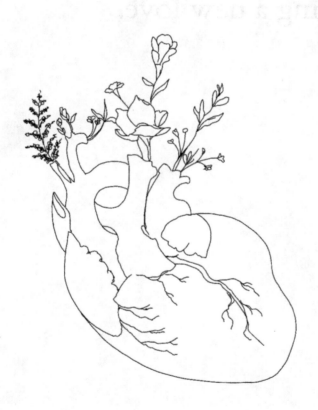

i should think my heart would know when it's you.
the glow around your figure as the rest of the room fades away.
the one.
yet, my heart has deceived me a million times before.
leaving me to question:
"what is the first sign + sight of love?"

love came in like an intoxicating tincture.
one drop on my tongue + i needed for nothing.

nervousness flutters at the core of our being.
the bitter taste of rejection
still lingers from our last chew.
reading the feedback of their behaviors,
their expressions,
their looks.
in attempts to conclude
the best response we could make.
is what we create here authentic + true?
or a simulation out of protection,
something to construe?

at the start we will filter what we want them to see,
a version of self we'd rather then be.
desire to be accepted,
we hide all our flaws.
with time comes experience
our true self it draws.
yet if we stand mid the discomfort
born of the initial unknowing,
confidently walk, the direction of unfolding.
we lean into the risk of potential rejection
therein lies the crux of true love + connection.

your presence infects me with the sick notion to give up my
control,
and fall recklessly to abandon.
in love.

-you are the sweetest drug

my mind composes novels around you, dear.
highlighting the perfection of everything you are.
everything we are.
casting fantasies of our union evolving.
a labor to anchor my mind here in the present.
that i might miss the sweet fragrance
that is the beginning.

a natural merging occurs in relationship.
lives overlap.
energies mingle.
mannerisms replicated.
friendships absorbed.
it's an art,
the balance of sacredness that is individuality,
and the sacredness that is the unit of two.

what is our voice tangled here in the mess?
picking out our truth from the knot.
differentiating ourselves as two separate people.
potential of activation in fear.

creating space does not equate distance.
but rather allows our lungs to fully breathe.
providing agency,
supporting consent.
through honesty
accepting influence,
of the wisdom shared by each being.

we fear the state of commitment.
the commitmentphobes are we.
wanting certainty to land on,
yet fear being caged permanently.

one foot in + one out
a constant to our game.
with the avoidance of commitment,
we sabotage each potential.
falling prey to distraction
that leads us tangential.

so to clarify + narrow
with the practice of intent,
we simplify the direction
and reduce our torment.

this is what i want.
i put forth into making.
saying with declaration.
my own undertaking.

but what if commitment
had less to do with the thing,
and more to do with the "we"?
the commitment to self
we believe we're unable,
a story it's selfish to be.
the balance
we strive for
'tween the self + each matter,
permits for a change
quieting inner chatter.

love expanded.

here we explore some of the unproductive definitions + common experiences that often arise in couples + individuals, which can block them from having healthy, operating relationships. from our early formative years, we begin an internal working model of how we see ourselves, others, + the world. these experiences define whether we believe we are deserving of love, or of having our needs met. we also grapple with the question of whether or not it comes to us under the conditions of something we do or become. as we grow, we gather new experiences that we deem either confirming of these original beliefs or challenge them to take on something new. ideally, we seek out mental constructs that lend to more liberation in terms of the way we exist in the world. constructs that provide acceptance + care for ourselves ensure greater likelihood we will not be destroyed in the process of living. these constructs allow others to extend care towards us + require a receptive response to let them. oftentimes, however, these constructs are not in place + we are left with the mental encumbrance of "not being enough," "being bad," or "not able to trust."

as human beings, we desire the experience of being met with receptivity + acceptance of our whole selves fearing a rejection that would put us out. at our core, we have the same human needs that can be summarized as "the six a's": attention, appreciation, affection, allowing, acceptance, + availability. when these are not adequately met, we resort to various strategies in order to have them met or "solutions" to protect us from the distressing experience of social disengagement. for example, if as children we sought connection through efforts of reaching out + eye contact only to be met with consistent misattuned or negative responses, we will form a prediction in our minds that reaching out will result in unpleasant consequences. moving forward, we won't reach out + perhaps care of our needs ourselves to protect against the distress of disengagement or rejection. further, we may even embody specific postures or automatic expressions that communicate the inner conflicting parts that desire their human needs to be met through another while also seeking to preserve the self from distress + harm. as we cast our partners as major sources for our needs to be met through, we are reminded of our own faults in the definition of love-- often imprinted from our initial primary caregivers + we unconsciously act in the ways that reflect this. even if those strategies are not healthy or conducive to intimacy.

we may be blind on the strategies we engage in to protect our sense of self, choosing safety over intimacy. yet we forget that, attached to the human body, we are relating to a human heart that feels just as strongly. we attempt to arrange the unfolding events through the stories of our minds, all the while sabotaging the potential of the very things we love about our partners: their agency + unique personhood. for example, we may have internalized at a young age that "love is conditional", receiving affection + praise only in times where we presented in a comical, entertaining manner. as we grow, we find ourselves presenting as the "life of the party" + having a hard time being authentic + vulnerable for fear that this risks losing our social engagement + security with others. the challenge here is that these strategies we engage in for preservation do not foster the intimacy required for sustaining healthy relationships. by making the conscious effort to untangle + understand the strategies we default to when in states of activation, we create the opportunity to reprogram ourselves with healthier options to choose from. the antidote to the fear that oftentimes infiltrates our minds lies in our active participation in the present moments, the positive aspects, + the compassionate perspectives. here, we are influenced to move towards our partner rather than away, or in pursuit of control.

our mission, if we choose to accept it, is to learn our own contribution to the dance we find ourselves in + ultimately identify more optimal skills for navigating our relationships. ideally we learn to tune into the self; connecting to our emotions, our thoughts + beliefs, our visceral body reactions, and our non-verbal communication-- so as to better create authenticity + congruency across our internal experience + expression of it.

emotion manifests in our body, showing up in auditory-visual mentalization + the felt senses-- where the emotional content generates in the body as the emotion plays out on the surface level of the body, through facial expressions. we all have a window of tolerance— should something exceed the threshold, the mind will begin to use strategies conditioned to regulate our nervous system response in the past. most of the time we apply "thinking," to a given situation, which shifts our processing to the past, in order to disconnect us from whatever the present, distressing stimuli may be.

ideally, as pack animals we regulate best when we are with others, feeling safe in a group, so we don't have to be hyper vigilant all the time. connection drives our sense of protection, therefore, co-regulation is key. yet, if we've never gotten into the practice of evaluating our actions and learning skills to override our automatic reactions after becoming dysregulated, most of us are still operating on the skill sets we learned in infancy.

with consistent work in the realm of mindfulness: of our actions, motivations, and feeling in our bodies-- we can attain effective functioning + healthy love, even if our internal alarm system goes off, wanting us to act in our default, conditioned strategies. we must be willing to learn the skills for when these alarm systems go off, in order to cope with them productively. for none of us were born knowing how to love, this is something we learn + continue to learn every day.

self-reflections:

1. in my childhood, are there memories of disappointments + rejections to asking for what i needed?
2. are there memories about conditions that i needed to meet in order to feel of worth or receive presence?
3. what did i believe my primary caregivers thought of me? did i receive messages that suggested i should be embarrassed? that i was weak if i showed emotion? that i did not matter? that i was bad or broken? that i was unsafe? that i was responsible for what happened in the family? that i was a burden or took too much energy to care for? that i did not deserve love? that i cannot trust the intentions of well-being from others?
4. what conclusions about love, intimacy, affection, trust, + dependency did i develop as a result of these memories?
5. how were these internalized beliefs about myself manifested + "validated" in romantic relationships moving forward?
6. how did i use my relationships to try + heal emotional injuries from my past?

yoga.

for it's in the practice of joining,
that we meet the parts we've been imploring.

on yamas + niyamas.

ahimsa.
compassion settles the mind who seeks to harm,
to blame,
to separate the being from the unifying whole.
the whole who collectively possesses the need to feel seen,
loved,
cared for.
our choices, a manifestation of the internal battles fought,
not a personal attack on ourselves,
but a projection.
where we struggle to hold the compassion to ourselves, we fail to
see the divinity.
to go about our lives with the intention of not harming others or
ourselves, we promote an innerpath that contributes to peaceful
existence.
when we can remember how the overextension of our selves only
exhausts our physical being, we can find balance in nourishment +
renewed energy for all.

satya.
truth on my tongue.
giving life to all I speak.
my voice,
the words that I choose,
painting someone's reality,
i'm indebted to keep.
connected i am that my dictation stays in resonance,
correcting the shift when I change up my stance.
that i don't unconsciously write a story not mine,
or lead you to a false impression over time.

asteya.
rooting from the belief of lack in our ability to meet ourselves,
we seek to steal therein from another.
"i am not enough" echos through the chambers of our mind,
infiltrating our perception
of our inherent perfection.
the perfection in the whole experience,
both the light + the dark,
allows us to revel in the truth of abundance.
rather than imprisoning ourselves to the chase + the cling of the
next pleasure,
aversion to anticipated pain if we were to slow ourselves down.

bramacharya.
conscious direction of our energy.
that leads us to our divinity.
down one path, we're left in lethargy
exhausting our bodies with unnecessary worry
exertion in presenting ourselves as someone we are not
to please,
to impress,
through endless attempts at being the best
rather than our best.
listening to the body, we forge a different path
one that fills us instead with vitality,
we find our prana
enriched + alive,
cultivating a life that serves us in our highest
conserving our powers for fulfillment.

aparigraha.
we immerse ourselves in the action of the journey,
as we release the attachment to the form of its fruits.
observant,
we become,
to the steady ebb + flow
of the impermanence existing therein.
as the bud opens to flower,
blessing sweet fragrance to our sky,
just as soon withdraws into her brown, fragile coat,
falling to the earth,
resigned.
should we attempt to hold on to the specifics of the design,
suffering we endure at the dissonance—
the creation of what we hold in our mind,
at odds with the physical manifestation.
we discover we've been absent to the joy of the journey,
the presence to the life while it had been living,
at which time we make a decision,
to hold on to what was,
continuing to live a story that now only exists in our hearts,
or let it flow on like a river on its own course.

saucha.
as the lotus emerges from the depths of the mud,
opening to the cool air,
pristine.
so do we rise out of the murky water that is judgment,
suggesting there are parts of us that are unclean.
the lotus cannot exist without the mud,
the purity is also our profanity.
where we radically accept our inherently impure self,
in all the real + messy components,
we come to the discovery that there is nothing left to purify.
the paradox that embraces it all as holy.

santosha.
i seek to become more of "myself"
through practices + templates designed by others.
the belief that satisfaction with who i am,
can be discovered in sacred fruit picked from outside.
i bite into the flesh as the juices drip down.
so certain the enjoyment is derived from this taste.
only to discover as i continue my journey moving forward,
the pleasure was always created within.

i rest in contentment.
satisfaction in my being.
we cannot love, trust, give or live fully until we have enough of that
love inside ourselves.

tapas.
where the path of our habit forges deep trails through our mind,
the friction generated by going against the grain sparks fire.
heat
in the very discipline it takes to refine ourselves.
burning away what no longer serves us,
what keeps us prisoner to our own, slow, destruction.
fervor
as we strive to be the best version of self that we can,
igniting + inspiring.
we find our way home.

svadhaya is the yogic principle of self- study. we practice this when we explore internally to seek out who we consider ourselves to be as individuals. we study our thoughts, feelings, behaviors + bodily reactions to understand our habits and thought processes. what happens when we do not create the space for ourselves to do so is we continue to run internal programs based on outdated belief systems that may not be serving us. yet they continue to influence our actions unconsciously.

no one.

is.

responsible.

for.

our.

actions.

except.

ourselves.

we try to blame our lover, our friend, our partner, our mother for circumstances, inner critical dialogue, our relationship patterns... however, when we do this we are stripping ourselves of our own power and suggesting we are not strong enough to take care of ourselves and our experience.

through self-observation + questioning, we come to understand the self, which in turn empowers the individual to embody the role of a creator in their own reality. writing their narrative, choosing their experience + feeling, partaking in the right action that aligns with their personal direction.

isvara pranidhana.
i surrender myself to divinity
the collective consciousness
and all of humanity.
relinquishing my hold
on the illusion of my control,
allowing it all to flawlessly unfold.

on the mat.

space allocated by the extent of my mat,
silence save the rhythm of my own breathing--
throat held in constriction,
oceanic sound reverberating through.
movement ensues
as i contract to expand.
ground + rebound.
pressure to release.
open + tight in.
the subtle lessons of clarity we receive only once quiet,
trickle down into consciousness.
the how.
the why.
the things we need to see.
elusive solutions inaccessible,
amid the chaos that is we.
with palm to the earth,
our weight shifting forward,
feeling our feet take flight.
we hold.
the patience we find—
the presence we foster—
the compassion we refine—
when we flow then in cadence
with intention to align.

to transition:
a need for time + space to changeover.
a decompression.
an emotional release.
a letting go.
we lean into the edge of our current self,
only to step into a new state of being.
should we rush ourselves faster than we are able,
creating disturbance, invalidation, + pain.
hold.
we perceive the change,
fear the change,
forcing the change to accelerate.
faster than our ability to allow + let go.
only to be met with resistance to let slow.
bringing us back to the process of transition
the process that's authentic
permitting us to grow.

the press of my hand
imprinting the mat.
rolling + arching
slow like a cat.
soft in each hold.
stillness in motion
mind in each fold,
body devotion.

on breathing.

over-zealous lungs.
work hard to meet the expectation
of the pictures fabricated by the mind.
fueling pressure,
stress.
fear.
as we effort to anchor ourselves back to what is here.
in presence
among the chaos that ensues.
we connect with this life pump to slow it all down.
discovering greater power as we do.
the sound of settling that takes on our hearts,
rhythmic beating,
we subdue.

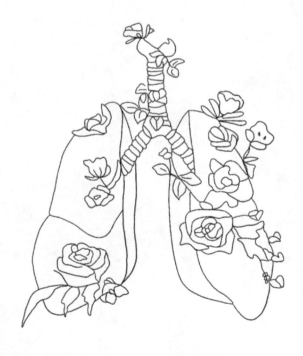

steady in
to steady out.
the rhythm of breathing does soothe.
clearing out the old,
to make space for the new,
revitalizing our system
a feeling we take to.

we can only inhale as deeply as we first exhale.

where does the breath travel,
when we invite it inside?
does it stay high in our hearts,
fluttering shallow + quick?
on mission so fast,
pumping in rhythm.
or does it sink deep into the belly,
down into to the pelvis,
circling around in the toes?
we present an image of the ever holy yogi,
yet do we allow the practice to penetrate?
a piercing of our living,
our body,
our essence,
our being.
or does it rest softly on the surface,
in a quiet state of perseverance
avoidant of anything that would ache,
that might challenge us
to awake.

where my lungs fill with the scent of the sky,
dissolving the ache that's within.
my soul sweeps up the fragments that erected the wall.
keeping love at a distance, therein.

the rhythm of the living air,
as it flows within your chest.
your active inhale breaths me in,
as my softened exhale takes you out.
weaving together our two energies,
like snakes that coil up around.
connecting us beyond these bodies,
while anchoring us to the ground.
my hand resting on your heart,
yours pressed so gently into mine.
the faint echo of a beat
steady cadence with perfect time.
lulls me into a living trance.
riding the waves of ecstatic rapture.
our souls commune in dance.

on intention.

an intention is not a destination,
but rather a point in which we start from.
giving us a direction to channel our efforts,
our focus.
laced through every word + thought + deed.
watch as we move energy from one place to another,
in attempt to resolve.
heal.
transform.
detached from the specific shape of outcome,
trusting it will unfold perfectly as it may:
"for where our attention goes,
our energy flows."
and all we can do is lead the way.

"bring me back to center."
the repeating words do order.
competing for real estate in the congestion of our mind.
causing a stalemate in our movement.
mantras to aid in the construction of more permanence,
in the construct of our higher knowing.
a remembrance to who we are beneath the bullshit,
a reclamation of ourselves as whole.
om mani padme hum.

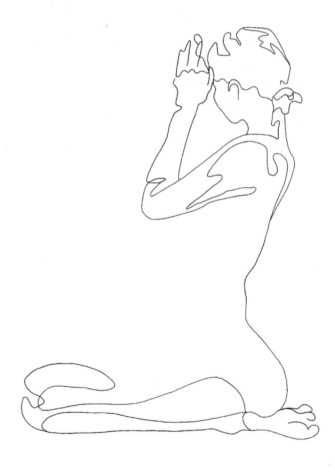

"light + love"
two words meant to encapsulate our work.
regurgitated by the mouths of teachers.
spoken with the intention,
to keep us in higher vibration,
unknowingly creating judgement in our thoughts.
designating a right versus wrong.
a good + a bad.
as if one is exclusive over another,
to reach the "enlightened" state.
no.
our work is not to coddle the lightness while disgusting at the dark,
but rather welcome in the dark to find the true light.
for it's not until we lay claim to the whole of each experience,
or take ownership to each part of our human,
can we truly begin to feel freedom.
an enlightened state remembers there is no wrong,
when everything is divine.
an enlightened state remembers there is no right,
when everything is one.

manifestation in words sets a direction.
manifestation in feeling brings out its success.

we hold immaculate dreams
of castles + kingdoms across the sky.
placing our thoughts + our intention
on something better to come by.
believing our greatest life exists for us
just beyond the veil.
the veil separating us from what we perceive is reality
and what we hold as a far-fetched fantasy.
and so it does.
disillusioned by what we believe is out there.
thinking it's the "thing" that will bring us the joy,
the peace,
the love,
the satisfaction.
only to discover it's not the "thing" at all.
this "thing" we've bet our whole life to
now feels meaningless + small.

before we pursue the manifestation of our desires,
we must first come to dissolve the illusions,
that continuously weigh us down.
the ones that tell us we are lacking.
the ones that say to do more,
be more,
have more.
rather than to realize
we already own the kingdom.
all we need to do is open
and receive it.

self-reflections:

1. where do i find my thoughts + desires drift to?
2. what beliefs do i have about myself in regards to my ability to realize them?
3. how do i see these beliefs impacting my behaviors + keeping me from realizing them?
4. what is one action i can take that helps alleviate the power of this belief on my taking action?

on the practice.

easy to get lost amid the flaws + complications of each thread.
yet when we zoom out to consume the entire tapestry,
we see the interwoven-- creating a beautiful, albeit painful,
masterpiece.

the mat sits rolled in dusty isolation.
where our eyes rove over,
no recognition.
lost amid the chaos of the mental train of thought.
avoidance of the practice,
as we are reminded of where we are not.
beliefs fill our minds
for our effort to be perfect,
execution of the practice
before we even start.
"practice"
no credence in the word.
as our egos fear the failure.
or the perception thereof.
cringing at the thought of the shaken beginner's start.
comparing ourselves to the capable seasoned heart.

rigidity.
the stiffness born out of stagnancy.
immobility.
fixed position.
perhaps we fear what comes with change.
frightened by the thought of being wrong.
frozen to the discomfort that arises.
plagued by the mistrust + surprises.
in ourselves.
in each other,
our tainted worldly view.
movement be our medicine,
dissolving the illness that ensues.
for it's in the presence of
the breath,
the stretch,
the discomfort,
the new
that we find space,
expansion,
freedom,
love.
and the ever expanding
you.

until one is committed,
the vultures of hesitancy + sabotage do appear.
swooping in to circle the meat of our labor,
picking at pieces
yet consuming very little.
leaving the remainder out to spoil
beneath the heat of the blazing sun.
until one is committed,
we hold the life
of the chance
to draw back.

so long as we do,
our energy + efforts bleed out.
what we are left with
is our ineffectiveness
and the bones of all our work
left bare.

creating space.
space in our hearts
space in our lives
space in our breath
space in our body

consciousness.
that what we then choose to fill here,
aligns us to a higher mind.

rituals hold space for transitions to unfold,
while honoring the life that once was.

if we believe our thoughts + feelings stay internal,
we are wrong.
as within, so without.
as above, so below.

on body love.

someone once told me: "we are not our bodies."
i clapped + i cheered.
how much truth to this statement.
oversaturated with messages to identify with our physical
imprisoning us to a specific ideal.
crippling us from a free + full expression of life.
so i denounced the body.
claimed i was free from the body.
consumed what i craved.
wore what i needed.
laid luxuriously around,
to everything i conceded.

i conceded.
not because it was something i desired,
but because i had grown weary + tired.
my bones ached
my mind a fog
my ambitions faded
my joy vanished.
not because it was something i desired,
but because my body had denounced me.
"we are not our bodies"
still we have a body.
we want to taste, we need a tongue.

we wish to breathe, we need our lungs.
we seek to feel, we need our hands.
the body holds our spirit, our life, our blood
we cannot exist one without another.

nurturing a relationship
where there's better balance + care
allows for us to taste
the juice this world has to share.

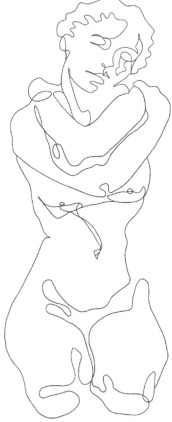

love be my teacher + show me the way.
to hold my body in exaltation,
care to keep revulsion at bay.

the shapes our bodies mold + make.
folding pieces
stretching lines.
like living origami we snake.
configurations
we refine.
sprawled across our floor we tangle
viewing outside from a different angle.
where breath meets heart meets rib meets hand.
moving in harmony, we expand.

in celebration to the whole.
the orchestration between the parts.
where oft we live in fragmentation.
competing our head versus our hearts.

in softened tones my lips preach your beauty
amid a world where criticism seems duty.
my flesh, my bones, my confidence is tested.
while in this light, all my self love attested.

on mindfulness.

in stillness,
we wait for that inner voice to arise.
as the outer world goes on to converse.
challenging what we see with our eyes
conviction, propriety in ways to transverse.
cutting through that blanketed noise,
coming to the faint whisper of truth.
requests the bravery to hold our poise,
undoing the programs of our youth.
voiced by our oft ignored body,
the delicate pleading soul.
craving our attention
seeking for us to be whole.

that space in between,
the richest landscape tenfold.
missed with our vision
cast on the end goal.
that space in between, each take of our breath.
between now + then later.
the beginning + old.
between novice + master.
selling + sold.
to slow + to savor
the process as it's done,
we invite all the juices
undiscovered
one-by-one.

wandering through a pathless forest,
where every tree appears like the last,
my steps seem aimless,
my roaming eyes directionless,
still i find myself
confidently lost.

unsure of the course.
being guided by a feeling.
no sense of orientation,
yet unbothered by the experience.
this quest has me discovering
tiny seedlings i'd never before to notice
aromatic clouds of sweet perfume
emitting from the luscious blooms.
cool earth to the pads of my feet,
grounding me in even deeper
with every step + every beat.

confidently lost,
little pressure to be found.
where my stroll becomes a journey
observing it all to be so profound.

how much more in love with our life we would be
if we decided to give ourselves no option,
except this moment we could see.

contemplation.
a strong, steady reflection.
carrying the bundle of analysis she's been loaded with.
absorbed in the abstract
making connections between the stars.
all to reveal an impressive painting.
she muses.
fantastical ideas.
scrawled across sheets to form exquisite landscapes of
stories + theories + suppositions.
a softened, yet secure smile settles over her face,
as the completion of this fine art comes to be.
reverence, from her audience,
to the complex texture + technique.
lost, for some, to the different storyline they extracted.

what power we convince ourselves we gain,
in the extravagant uncovering of the "truth".
only to recognize this power can disconnect us,
preventing trust,
empathy,
intimacy,
and the love of you.

on flow.

changing environments move so quickly.
we barely breathe before they're gone.
yet it's in our ability to adapt,
react.
our fluidity
that captures us before we fall.
what is our spine?
smooth gliding snake in their crawl,
silken, ease like liquid,
amid
the earthly drawl.
or is it tight, tense, + rigid
grasping, clinging at it all?
defending some internal reality,
that hesitation breeds the fall.

to flow given structure,
can allow for freedom
within the established edge.

stagnancy.
with the cessation of movement,
the only thing that can grow is toxic
for our minds + bodies to consume.

the dissolving of ego,
as a vibrant energy takes us over.
single focus + absorption to the activity we partake.
peace fills our hearts,
enraptured by this minute
connected to all that is me, is you, is this, is we.
time contorts beyond all recognition,
getting lost,
changing shape,
jumping lines,
as we escape.
flow state.
a desirous condition
like drugs to our system.
the pure presence of life in its fullest enjoyment.
fleeting,
as our action comes to completion,
we leave in a glow.
gently slipping from our fingers
sand we try to hold.
until we find that next state of concentration.
the escape from all the others,
or perhaps it's an invitation
the inclusion of all.
recognizing the wholeness
no matter how small.

on surrender + letting go.

to surrender,
we melt
into that which causes contraction.
annoyance.
irritation.
fear.
choosing to let it co-exist.
allowing it to have time to be here.

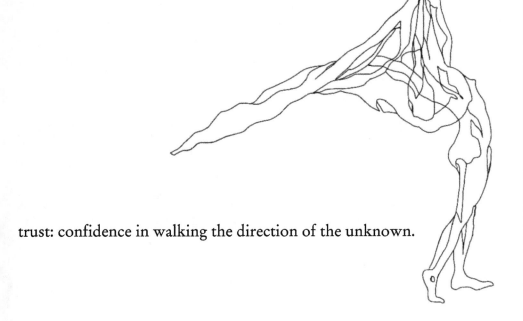

trust: confidence in walking the direction of the unknown.

"i'm barely holding on."
our fantasy stops at the worst part of the narrative.
imagining our darkest hour.
yet if we allow the story of our minds to unfold here,
seeing it through to the end—
we discover a point that is much less dense.
and our hope in potential can emerge.

curiosity.
a biological motivational system,
that fuels our innate desire to investigate
what's novel + ambiguous.
when we can embody the power of curiosity—
directed to ourselves,
our lover,
a situation—
we become inspired,
as we see it all anew.
expanding our potential in every direction,
rewriting our script from everything we knew.

the dogs of indecision,
racing across the yard.
back + forth full of zeal
they go.
for whatever reason,
no one could know.
discomfort rests in the agitation,
when we feel we are stuck
in the process of the question.
holding two potentials that don't exist,
except for here in our mind.
fearing the responsibility to outcome,
should it fall far from the line.
to give the question space.
attention
to reveal
the countering voices that spurn in our head,
we give life to our parts,
recognizing what is said.
acceptance
to feel
their efforts to protect us
based from every past ordeal.
to surrender to the process,
making a commitment then to choose
or allow.
breaks us free of the incessant chase,
bringing us back to the "now."

timelessness.
it's only in the resistance that makes us aware of the passing hour.

self-reflection:

1. what is a current question i find myself in?
2. what is a question i have about the question that i find myself in?
3. what are the potential outcomes i entertain could happen?
4. what resources do i have available to me that would help me survive + thrive in either potential outcome?
5. do i trust my ability to take care of myself in either situation?

on meditation.

allowing our eyelids to close to the image of the vast world that lay
before us.
leaving us in the cool, calm darkness
of ourselves.

drawing the cherished breath deep, down, into our bodies,
feeling it touch us,
awaken us, from within.
saturating our vessel,
nourishing our existence.

as we exhale, we feel the weight of responsibility, guilt, shame,
inadequacy,
fall from our shoulders,
to be absorbed by the earth.
no longer ours to carry,
we surrender.

should any unresolved feelings arise, we allow the feelings to be
present.
permission for us to feel them,
see them,
hear them,
while witnessing them continue to go their own way out.
settling back into stillness with complete + loving kindness.
as we practice our welcome,
to our whole state of being.

time melts like ice
beneath the fiery, radiant sun.
wetting the earth only to evaporate,
vanishing 'til there's none.
we watch in awe + wonderment
"where does it all go?"
this time.
when we are lost to the absorption of our own attention.
to that space in between each minute
the one that rests before + the one that sits there after.
so fleeting,
the only one we truly have,
yet, it's the one too fast for us to hold on.
"now" they call it.
the holy grail of healing.
of freedom.
finding the answer in all the feeling.
what is alive
in our hearts
giving direction
to where to start.

the original sound,
that carries all vibration throughout the universe.
uplifting + transmuting the soul
as it harmonizes with the world around us.
in light + truth,
we discover.
ohm.

certainty is the death of growth.
but curiosity births infinity.

who am i?
a repeated question i am after.
the power in that one single line
settles down all mental chatter.

drunk on my own ego.
sweet honey to my lips.
checking in for validation
your words—
intoxicating hit.
getting high off my pride.
believing my words speak in wisdom.
lucid to the notion
that it's all divine,
unassisted.
to allude there's no separation,
between myself + what is all.
would be to accept on some fucked level
this doesn't matter,
not at all.
although,
to drop the matter,
to release the care.
to see myself
in everyone,
everywhere.
might relieve this incessant bickering, i hear.
the back + forth between the ears
that threatens my place in worldly value
my constant companion, to all these years.
a pause in the pressure to feel caught up.
tempting to my weary soul.
would require me to give it up
what i believed was mine to control.

as i breathe in:
so.
as i breathe out:
hum.
one with the universal-consciousness.
illusion to the separateness.
the space in between,
nothing,
but myself.

- *i am that*

eliminating mental distraction,
as i focus on a single thought.
word.
action.
sound—
that reverberates through my body.
a gong echoes through the chambers of my heart,
destruction to any illusion that takes residence.
walls collapse that have protected me
imprisoned me
captive to my own freedom.
the taste of that first sweet breath
as it fills the space in my liberated lungs,
nourishes me like life-giving water
saturating the cracks of the parched earth.

the incessant creature that prowled around my head in hunger.
seeking for everything to fill him
or anything.
i doubt he even knew.
reaching + racing
sonsuming + pacing.

i ask: what is this craving that you feel?
the creature snarled as if I should know this.
back to his pacing, in search for a new meal.

the longer the question laid out in the air,
the slower the creature became.
as his attention to the hunger challenged his impulse.
making conscious to the incessant, the end that never came.

tired of the chase,
he came back to me with a plea.
fatigue + sadness he wore like a cape.
as he asked whatever he could then do.
i peered into his big ferocious eyes,
holding them
loving them
breathing them in

and as a soft smile settled over his face,
i knew my work had been done.
"you may go"
the creature stepped back, puzzled + amazed.
quietly he wandered off,
as if in a daze.
his hunger never becoming voracious again.
feeling satiated, whole.
never wanting more therein.

in the still water,
we peer our reflection,
a fine mirror to observe + give our introspection.
quiet reverence,
as we hold our own gaze.
a promise to love us
for all of our days.
as our focus shifts to beyond the reflection,
we take note of the bustling life there below
a world beneath the surface we'd never notice existed
ahould stillness + contemplation not be our teachers.

self-reflections:

1. what activities do i find the experience of "losing myself" in flow + enjoyment?
2. what time + attention do i give to these activities in my life?
3. if there are blocks preventing me from creating space for these, what can i do to mitigate them?

yoga expanded.

yoga, in sanskrit, means "to yoke" or "to join". indeed, this practice brings together the various facets of hindu philosophy, combining a rich tradition of both mental + physical practices which are designed to achieve optimal health of the body + mind. yoga is typically taught through what is called the "eight limbs"-- each one describing a path to bringing oneself closer to union with oneself + the universe surrounding. the eight limbs include: *yama* (abstinences), *niyama* (observances), *asana* (postures), *pranayama* (breath control), *pratyahara* (withdrawal of the senses), *dharana* (concentration), *dhyana* (meditation) and *samadhi* (absorption). for the practitioner, these practices guide them through a process of interrupting the default programming of their mind + body to bring them into a role of conscious choice of action + physical system regulation.

the *yamas* + *niyamas* are ethical principles to living one's life in relationship to others + how we take care of ourselves. the five yamas describe social restraint + invite us to avoid violence, non-truthfulness, stealing, wasting energy, and possessiveness. the five niyamas are self-disciplines that ask us to engage in acts of cleanliness + contentment, purify ourselves with heat + passion in our discipline, embrace self-study through observation of our thoughts + actions, + surrender to a power greater than ourselves. contemplation of how we relate to ourselves + others helps to promote greater peace of mind + adds calmness to our lives.

asana is usually translated as "pose" or "posture" + refers to the physical practice of connecting to the body where we develop the habit of discipline + ability to concentrate. when we practice yoga asana, we are drawing awareness into our body. as we flow between poses, our body reacts to the perception of the strain that arises from the position. here, we observe the automatic thoughts, the sensations, the changes of breath, the emotions that are elicited. for example, we lift one foot from the floor + are instructed to extend it forward in balance. the body begins to shake under the strain of the muscles engaging to keep the body upright. the mind begins to chatter: "this is so hard. i'm bad at this." the body's stress response kicks in, reacting to the distress of the mind, as our heart + breath quicken. consequently, the body begins to shake more + we may fall over. this observation brings us into power of what factors are comprising each experience so we may more easily take charge in determining a more effective way of responding. when we combine the asana practice with pranayama, we gain greater control over the physical response.

pranayama teaches us to maximize the flow of oxygen throughout our bodies in order to alleviate stress, increase mental focus, regulate the nervous system, increase blood circulation, and deepen relaxation. consciously matching breath to body movement helps regulate the mind-body connection of our autonomic nervous system, strengthening our ability to consciously manage the automatic responses of the body to perceived stress. here we develop the ability to self-regulate + bring ourselves back to center + to calm. so instead of losing our balance out of criticism, we observe the thought, + remind ourselves, "i am safe. this discomfort will pass," we slow down our breathing, + relax the tension building in the body, and we find that our experience in the posture changes. we find that we can hold the position for longer or that our physiological response to it becomes more tolerable.

pratyahara is the practice of withdrawing ourselves from actively participating in the world without completely losing contact with it. this is where we rest in stillness, registering the sounds + sensations that are occurring around us, but not creating any mental or physical disturbance or engagement with it. we experience a non-reaction. we are in the world, but not of it.

the last three limbs are associated with the internal experience of the practitioner, helping them to separate the activities of the mind independent from the physical senses. d*harana* is the binding of our conscious awareness to a single point. these are the mindfulness exercises that utilize single-focused awareness, such as focus on breath, body sensations, mantras, chakras, or drishti--a softened focus of the eyes on a single external point, to aid us in the regulation of our mind's processes. when we can concentrate strongly, the chatter + noise of the mind tend to fall away. there is less space for the mind to plan, organize, analyze. the mind becomes peaceful which in turn makes other aspects of our lives easier. dharana helps us to observe the patterns of the mind so we may more easily interrupt unhelpful thought patterns that might lead to undesirable outcomes and behavior. overtime, this practice reduces the busy chattering monkey mind that ruled our mental space before.

dhyana, or meditation, involves achieving a state of "thoughtless awareness". it is the continuation of dharana as our state of concentration matures. here, the point lies on the intention of knowing the truth about the subject in focus. this deeper concentration provides self-knowledge where one can separate illusion from reality. we experience this state when we become mesmerized + lost in the concentration of an activity while the rest of the world + time falls away. we can experience this in activities like surfing, driving, drawing, writing or any other state that creates "flow".

we reach *samadhi,* or the state of enlightenment, when we become completely absorbed into the object we concentrate + the space surrounding it. here, our process of concentration, the object of concentration, and the mind that is doing the concentration have all become one + we can no longer discern any separation. in other words, we become only aware of the essence of divinity + our relationship to it, while all detail to form fall away.

as explained, yoga is a holistic practice that brings balance to one's life. as a regular part of one's lifestyle, yoga can help the relationship between the body + mind to function at its greatest potential, encouraging a relaxed state of being, which is highly conducive to the health + satisfaction of our relationships + even our sex life.

all together now.

change is inevitable, as the impermanence of every feeling, person, day, and season transitions to bring forth a new way of relating to it. whether this relationship be a birth, a maturation, or a death, how we perceive + engage with it becomes something new. suffering is inevitable, as we compare the perfection of our idealized minds to the variable reality that lies before us. as much as we'd like to believe that both of these can be controlled by our own efforts, we feel the discomfort as we press into the resistance of the flow to stop it from coming.

as a collective, we share in this human experience + the many desires, needs + fears that make it up. in pursuit of what will bring us into peace + safety, we navigate the world with the best of what we know, using the perceptions + rules we have been given. to deny that we are any different than the fellow man around us would be to deny parts of ourselves we'd rather not own. on the path of being human, we come to face trials that challenge the very foundations of what we believe to be true. dissonance to our cognitions cause us to question what is real. when we take these moments of resistance + contemplate their meaning + purpose for us, we empower ourselves to become the rightful creators of our own reality.

evolution is determined by the efforts made to not fight against resistance, but rather to go along with it + adapt to change in the environment for optimal survival. when we become consciously aware of the forces at play, separating our own identity from the part of us that reacts + the outcomes that unfold, we can more efficiently + effectively determine practices that take us in the direction of our hearts, with more ease.

as we grow from being small children into adulthood, we rely on the practices instilled from our parents to develop our minds + response to the world. the rituals + habits, or lack thereof, that ruled their lives, become our first reference to understanding our role + power in the events of this world. practices like yoga help us to develop + strengthen those skills that we may have not been gifted with early in life. It gives us structure + direction to funnel our efforts into evolving beyond the stories of our childhood wounds, helping us to recognize our own power to change circumstances. in yoga, we learn that our thoughts + our bodies + our actions do not determine the worth or identity of who we are, but rather, can be consciously used in ways to promote our liberation from external forces + happenstance. as a result, we find that our relationships + self become more liberated. we can finally find the peace, both physically + mentally, that we've been searching for all our lives.

without awareness we continue to be unconscious to the beliefs that shape our everyday lives. without discipline we continue to live out our patterns, repeating the same outcomes we had the day before. without surrender, we continue to press on, though our bodies and life instances may create resistance. without a positive relationship to our bodies, we lose out on an intelligence that seeks to help us. without sexuality, we disconnect ourselves from the very essence of our natural being. without love, we forget the interconnectedness of us all. we can exist in the world, one without the other, but once we get that first taste of the nekter that drips, as essence of the flower, why would we want to? it is in these realizations + practices that we connect to that which is bigger than ourselves, finding greater purpose to our existence. we finally comprehend the purpose of our practice + lessons of our teachers: although we feel lonely, we are never alone. not when the world continues to breathe of the same human existence, thoughts, emotions + questions.

this is what it feels like to be in our bodies, in our hearts, of every soul, in union.
welcome home.

notes.

1. May, Rollo (1975). *The courage to create.* Viking.
2. Frankl, V. E. (1984). *Man's search for meaning: An introduction to logotherapy.* Simon & Schuster.
3. Greening, T. (2018) Holocaust poems: A gentile's perspective. Garden Wall Publishers.
4. Greening, T. (2020). Into the void: An existential psychologist faces death through poetry. University Professors Press.
5. Greening, T. (2011). Sartre? Not smart. *Humanistic Psychologist,* 39(1), 64-64.
6. O'Sullivan N, Davis P, Billington J, Gonzalez-Diaz V, Corcoran R. (2015). Shall I compare thee: The neural basis of literary awareness, and its benefits to cognition. *Cortex,* 73(1), 44-157.

dr cat meyer, psyd is a psychotherapist + published researcher specializing in sex + relationships. through her books, podcasts, international speaking, + retreats she demonstrates a dedication to evolving the relationships + conversations we have around sex + our bodies.

her decades of self-inquiry + personal development through teachings of yoga, embodiment, tantra, psychology, + energetics have cultivated a deeper understanding of all the complex ways we as humans operate + move towards healing.

dr cat believes in the medicine of art + poetry to heal. she's an avid practitioner for igniting the wildish ways, harnessing the power of sensuality, + befriending the intelligence of the body for greater intuition + healthy love.

through her writing and illustrations, dr cat explores themes of love, loss, heartbreak, trauma, healing, embodiment, sex, identity, and the relationships we have with our own bodies.

sexloveyoga.com
@sexloveyoga

dear reader,

thank you for savoring my poetic words on your tongue. i hope it brings you the inspiration + validation to bravely step forward on your path in sex, love, + yoga.

to further support you on your journey, i have free resources around sensuality, sexuality, + embodiment available to you on my website at sexloveyoga.com

may you continue to nurture the lovership with your body + commit to learning how to listen from the inside.

with that said, writing + creating art is my passion as much as it is the medium through which i share my insights of the world. in order for my words to find the ears that need to hear them, the internet uses reviews as a way to boost visibility. my heart would be in deep gratitude if you were to write a review on amazon + share with your friends + loved ones. in exchange, i will promise to continue writing + creating just for you.

in love + play,
dr cat

CPSIA information can be obtained
at www.ICGtesting.com
Printed in the USA
LVHW021255280222
712195LV00009B/434